14 Days Prayer

for

Uncommon

Miracles

TIMOTHY ATUNNISE

TSA SOLUTION PUBLISHING
ATLANTA, GEORGIA

UNCOMMON MIRACLES

GLOVIM PUBLICATIONS
1078 Citizens Pkwy
Suite A
Morrow, Georgia 30260
glovimbooks@gmail.com
www.glovimonline.org

TSA Solution Publishing
A division of Timat Store, LLC.
Atlanta, GA 30294
timatstore@yahoo.com

Cover Design: Tim Atunnise

IMPORTANT NOTICE

Deliverance is a benefit of the Kingdom, only for the children of God. If you have not accepted Jesus Christ as your personal Lord and Savior, this is the best time to do so.

Before you continue, you need to be sure you are in the right standing with God if you want to exercise authority and power in the name of Jesus Christ. The Bible says,
"Then he called his twelve disciples together, and gave them power and authority over all devils, and to cure diseases." - Luke 9:1

"And these signs shall follow them that believe; in my name shall they cast out devils; they shall speak with new tongues; they shall take up serpents; and if they drink any deadly thing, it shall not hurt them; they shall lay hands on the sick, and they shall recover." – Mark 16:17-18.

These are promises for the Children of God, not just for everyone. Why don't you give your life to Christ today and you will have access to the same promises. Food that is meant for the children will not be given to the dogs.

"But he answered and said, it is not meet to take the children's bread, and cast it to dogs" – Matthew 15:26.

If you really want to be delivered from any bondage of the wicked and be set free from any form of captivity, I ask you today to give your life to Christ. If you are ready, say this prayer with all your heart:

4

"Dear Heavenly Father, You have called me to Yourself in the name of Your dear Son Jesus Christ. I realize that Jesus Christ is the only Way, the Truth, and the Life.

I acknowledge to You that I am a sinner. I believe that Your only begotten Son Jesus Christ shed His precious blood on the cross, died for my sins, and rose again on the third day. I am truly sorry for the deeds which I have committed against You, and therefore, I am willing to repent (turn away from my sins). Have mercy on me, a sinner. Cleanse me, and forgive me of my sins.

I truly desire to serve You, Lord Jesus. Starting from now, I pray that You would help me to hear Your still small voice. Lord, I desire to be led by Your Holy Spirit so I can faithfully follow You and obey all of Your commandments. I ask You for the strength to love You more than anything else so I won't fall back into my old ways. I also ask You to bring genuine believers into my life who will encourage me to live for You and help me stay accountable.

Jesus, I am truly grateful for Your grace which has led me to repentance and has saved me from my sins. By the indwelling of Your Holy Spirit, I now have the power to overcome all sin which before so easily entangled me. Lord Jesus, please transform my life so that I may bring glory and honor to You alone and not to myself.

Right now I confess Jesus Christ as the Lord of my life. With my heart, I believe that God the Father raised His Son Jesus Christ from the dead. This very moment I acknowledge that Jesus Christ is my Savior and according to His Word, right now I am born again. Thank You Jesus, for coming into my life and hearing my prayer. I ask all of this in the name of my Lord and Savior, Jesus Christ. Amen".

I hereby congratulate and welcome you into the Kingdom. You hereby have full access to the benefits, promises and blessings of the Kingdom.

This book is loaded with blessings, you will not be disappointed as you continue to enjoy the goodness of the Lord.

INSTRUCTIONS

If you are new to this method of prayer, please follow this instruction carefully:

Step 1:

Spend enough time in praising and worshiping God not just for what He is about to do or what He has done, but WHO HE IS.

Step 2:

Unforgiveness will surely hinder your prayer, take time to remember all those who have done you wrong, and forgive them from the bottom of your heart. THIS IS VERY IMPORTANT BECAUSE YOUR DELIVERANCE DEPENDS ON IT.

Step 3:

Believe in your heart that God will answer your prayer when you call upon Him, and do not doubt in your heart.

Step 4:

Pray in the name of Jesus Christ alone.

Step 5:

Repeat each prayer point 25 to 30 times or until you are convinced that you receive answer before you go to the next prayer point. Example: When you take prayer point number 1, you say this prayer over and over again, 25 – 30 times or until you are convinced that you have an answer before you go to prayer point number 2.

Step 6:

It will be more effective if you can fast along with your prayer. If you want total deliverance from your bondage, take 3 days of sacrifice in fasting as you say your prayer aggressively, asking your situation to receive permanent solution and YOUR DELIVERANCE WILL BE MADE PERFECT IN THE NAME OF JESUS CHRIST. AMEN!

Table of Contents

But this kind does not go out except by prayer and fasting.
-    Matthew 17:21

DAY ONE

IT IS TIME FOR A CHANGE

Passages To Read Before You Pray:
Isaiah 42:13, Joshua 6:7, Exodus 3:7-8,
Psalms 86, 42, 44, 19, 69

In the book of Job 22:28, the Scripture says when I decree a thing, it shall be established for me. I stand on this Scripture and decree. I have come into the presence of God today to plead my case. I enter through the gate of praise, into the sanctuary of heaven. I cover myself in the precious blood of Jesus Christ. I baptize myself in the fire of the Holy Ghost. I charge this atmosphere with the fire of God, and I take this neighborhood for the Lord. I arrest every principality and power, territorial spirit, and every throne and kingdom that is not of God. I cast you down and I command you never to lift yourself up against me, because I have the life of God in me.

In the name of Jesus Christ, I confess my sins today, and I ask you O Lord to forgive me on the basis of your mercy. With all my heart, I forgive those who have sinned against me; from the past through this moment. I release them from any form of guilt and shame, in the name of Jesus Christ. I hereby plead the blood of Jesus over any sins committed by my parents and ancestors. I cancel through the Blood of Jesus Christ, any satanic covenants, exchanges, vows or transactions, made over my life, body, soul, spirit, and circumstances, in the name of Jesus Christ. I cancel every legal right that the devil may have against me, by the blood of Jesus Christ. The accuser of the brethren will have nothing against me, as I come to the presence of God in prayer.

The devil cannot hinder or delay my prayer, because I know who I am. I am a child of the Kingdom. I am a king and priest of the Lord, redeemed from the hand of the devil by the blood of Jesus Christ. I walk in power. I walk in miracle. Proverbs 18:21 says, death and life are in the power of my tongue; I command the power in my tongue to manifest now. I command my tongue to become fire, to consume all the powers of darkness in the air, the land, the sea, and beneath the earth. I hereby raise Holy Ghost standard against the prince of the power of the air and all the hosts of darkness in the air. I raise Holy Ghost standard against the queen of the coasts and all the hosts of darkness on the land. I raise Holy Ghost standard against the marine kingdom and all the hosts of darkness in the sea. I raise Holy Ghost standard against the kingdom of hell and all the hosts of darkness beneath the earth. I shoot down all the networks of demons gathering to resist my prayers. I rebuke and bind all the controlling forces of darkness standing against my prayers.

I declare that all satanic thrones, altars, dominions, principalities, powers, rulers of darkness, queens of the coast, queens of heavens, household wickedness, spiritual hosts of wickedness and all satanic works, have no power or authority over my life. I declare that satanic harassment and intimidation have no effect on me.

Today, I receive divine strength to pray; I will not pray in vain. I will not pray amiss. My prayers will bring the desired results. I command the fountain of prayer to open now, and to flow into my life, I command the warring angels of God to descend and fight on my behalf. Every minute and every hour that I spend in prayer, will bring solution. Every prayer point will attract divine attention and divine intervention. I decree open heavens over my

prayers, and today, God of heaven and earth will attend to my case. My prayers today will shake the heavens and move the earth. Testimonies, miracles, healings, breakthroughs, and signs and wonders, will follow my prayers. At the end of this prayer session, my life will never be the same again.

PRAYER POINTS

1. O God my Father, thank you for being my God, my Father and my friend.
2. O God my Father, thank you for the privilege to know you and the power of the resurrection of Jesus Christ.
3. O God my Father, thank you for always being there for me and with me.
4. O God my Father, thank you for the great and mighty things that you are doing in my life.
5. O God my Father, thank you for your provision and protection over me and my household.
6. O God my Father, thank you for always answering my prayers.
7. I confess my sins before you today and I ask you to forgive me on the basis of your mercy, in the name of Jesus Christ.
8. Wash me clean today O Lord by the blood of Jesus Christ.
9. I cover myself and my household with the blood of Jesus Christ.
10. My prayers today will not go in vain; my prayers will produce the desired results in the name of Jesus Christ.
11. I stand on the Word of God. I command great things to manifest in my life, in the name of Jesus Christ.

12. I stand on the Word of God. I command great things to manifest in my home, in the name of Jesus Christ.

13. I stand on the Word of God. I command great things to manifest in every area of my life, in the name of Jesus Christ.

14. I stand on the Word of God. I command great things to manifest in my marriage, in the name of Jesus Christ.

15. I stand on the Word of God. I command great things to manifest in my finances, in the name of Jesus Christ.

16. I stand on the Word of God. I command great things to manifest in my family, in the name of Jesus Christ.

17. I stand on the Word of God. I command great things to manifest in my business, in the name of Jesus Christ.

18. I stand on the Word of God. I command great things to manifest in my ministry, in the name of Jesus Christ.

19. I stand on the Word of God. I decree progress into every area of my life, in the name of Jesus Christ.

20. I stand on the Word of God. I decree progress upon the works of my hands, in the name of Jesus Christ.

21. I stand on the Word of God. I decree progress into my spiritual life, in the name of Jesus Christ.

22. I stand on the Word of God. I decree progress into my prayer life, in the name of Jesus Christ.

23. In Psalm 105:37, the Bible says, He brought them forth also with silver and gold: and there was not one feeble person among their tribes. Arise O Lord and take away my pains. You are the Lord that heals me, in the name of Jesus Christ.

24. In Psalm 105:37, the Bible says, He brought them forth also with silver and gold: and there was not one feeble person among their tribes. Arise O Lord and take away my sickness. You are the Lord that heals me, in the

name of Jesus Christ.

25. In Psalm 105:37, the Bible says, He brought them forth also with silver and gold: and there was not one feeble person among their tribes. Arise O Lord and take away my infirmities. You are the Lord that heals me, in the name of Jesus Christ.

26. In Psalm 105:37, the Bible says, He brought them forth also with silver and gold: and there was not one feeble person among their tribes. Arise O Lord and take away my headaches. You are the Lord that heals me, in the name of Jesus Christ.

27. In Psalm 105:37, the Bible says, He brought them forth also with silver and gold: and there was not one feeble person among their tribes. Arise O Lord and take away my high blood pressure. You are the Lord that heals me, in the name of Jesus Christ.

28. In Psalm 105:37, the Bible says, He brought them forth also with silver and gold: and there was not one feeble person among their tribes. Arise O Lord and take away my low blood pressure. You are the Lord that heals me, in the name of Jesus Christ.

29. In Psalm 105:37, the Bible says, He brought them forth also with silver and gold: and there was not one feeble person among their tribes. Arise O Lord and take away my diabetes. You are the Lord that heals me, in the name of Jesus Christ.

30. In Psalm 105:37, the Bible says, He brought them forth also with silver and gold: and there was not one feeble person among their tribes. Arise O Lord and take away my joint pains. You are the Lord that heals me, in the name of Jesus Christ.

31. In Psalm 105:37, the Bible says, He brought them forth

also with silver and gold: and there was not one feeble person among their tribes. Arise O Lord and take away my back pains. You are the Lord that heals me, in the name of Jesus Christ.

32. In Psalm 105:37, the Bible says, He brought them forth also with silver and gold: and there was not one feeble person among their tribes. Arise O Lord and take away my hip pains. You are the Lord that heals me, in the name of Jesus Christ.

33. In Psalm 105:37, the Bible says, He brought them forth also with silver and gold: and there was not one feeble person among their tribes. Arise O Lord and take away my menstrual pains. You are the Lord that heals me, in the name of Jesus Christ.

34. In Psalm 105:37, the Bible says, He brought them forth also with silver and gold: and there was not one feeble person among their tribes. Arise O Lord and take away my stomach pains. You are the Lord that heals me, in the name of Jesus Christ.

35. In Psalm 105:37, the Bible says, He brought them forth also with silver and gold: and there was not one feeble person among their tribes. Arise O Lord and take away cancer from my body. You are the Lord that heals me, in the name of Jesus Christ.

36. In Psalm 105:37, the Bible says, He brought them forth also with silver and gold: and there was not one feeble person among their tribes. Arise O Lord and take away every developmental disability. You are the Lord that heals me, in the name of Jesus Christ.

37. In Psalm 105:37, the Bible says, He brought them forth also with silver and gold: and there was not one feeble person among their tribes. Arise O Lord and take away

every form of health disorder. You are the Lord that heals me, in the name of Jesus Christ.

38. In Psalm 105:37, the Bible says, He brought them forth also with silver and gold: and there was not one feeble person among their tribes. Arise O Lord and take away every form of health problem. You are the Lord that heals me, in the name of Jesus Christ.

39. In Psalm 105:37, the Bible says, He brought them forth also with silver and gold: and there was not one feeble person among their tribes. Arise O Lord and take away my eye problems. You are the Lord that heals me, in the name of Jesus Christ.

40. In Psalm 105:37, the Bible says, He brought them forth also with silver and gold: and there was not one feeble person among their tribes. Arise O Lord and take away my hearing problem. You are the Lord that heals me, in the name of Jesus Christ.

41. In Psalm 105:37, the Bible says, He brought them forth also with silver and gold: and there was not one feeble person among their tribes. Arise O Lord and take away my heart problem. You are the Lord that heals me, in the name of Jesus Christ.

42. In Psalm 105:37, the Bible says, He brought them forth also with silver and gold: and there was not one feeble person among their tribes. Arise O Lord and take away my kidney problem. You are the Lord that heals me, in the name of Jesus Christ.

43. In Psalm 105:37, the Bible says, He brought them forth also with silver and gold: and there was not one feeble person among their tribes. Arise O Lord and take away my liver problem. You are the Lord that heals me, in the name of Jesus Christ.

44. In Psalm 105:37, the Bible says, He brought them forth also with silver and gold: and there was not one feeble person among their tribes. Arise O Lord and take away my skin problem. You are the Lord that heals me, in the name of Jesus Christ.

45. In Psalm 105:37, the Bible says, He brought them forth also with silver and gold: and there was not one feeble person among their tribes. Arise O Lord and take away my brain tumor. You are the Lord that heals me, in the name of Jesus Christ.

46. In Psalm 105:37, the Bible says, He brought them forth also with silver and gold: and there was not one feeble person among their tribes. Arise O Lord and take away fibroids in my uterus. You are the Lord that heals me, in the name of Jesus Christ.

47. In Psalm 105:37, the Bible says, He brought them forth also with silver and gold: and there was not one feeble person among their tribes. Arise O Lord and take away every problem in my lungs. You are the Lord that heals me, in the name of Jesus Christ.

48. In Psalm 105:37, the Bible says, He brought them forth also with silver and gold: and there was not one feeble person among their tribes. Arise O Lord and take away every problem in my intestines. You are the Lord that heals me, in the name of Jesus Christ.

49. In Psalm 105:37, the Bible says, He brought them forth also with silver and gold: and there was not one feeble person among their tribes. Arise O Lord and take away cancer in my bones. You are the Lord that heals me, in the name of Jesus Christ.

50. In Psalm 105:37, the Bible says, He brought them forth also with silver and gold: and there was not one feeble

person among their tribes. Arise O Lord and take away every diagnosed sickness in my body. You are the Lord that heals me, in the name of Jesus Christ.

51. In Psalm 105:37, the Bible says, He brought them forth also with silver and gold: and there was not one feeble person among their tribes. Arise O Lord and take away every undiagnosed sickness in my body. You are the Lord that heals me, in the name of Jesus Christ.

52. In Psalm 105:37, the Bible says, He brought them forth also with silver and gold: and there was not one feeble person among their tribes. Arise O Lord and take away every of my health problems. You are the Lord that heals me, in the name of Jesus Christ.

53. In Exodus 23:25, the Bible says, you shall serve the LORD your God, and He will bless your bread and your water, and I will take sickness away from among you. O God my Father, you are Jehovah Rapha, take away every sickness from my life, in the name of Jesus Christ.

54. In Exodus 23:25, the Bible says, you shall serve the LORD your God, and He will bless your bread and your water, and I will take sickness away from among you. O God my Father, you are Jehovah Rapha, take away every sickness from the life of my spouse, in the name of Jesus Christ.

55. In Exodus 23:25, the Bible says, you shall serve the LORD your God, and He will bless your bread and your water, and I will take sickness away from among you. O God my Father, you are Jehovah Rapha, take away every sickness from the lives of my children, in the name of Jesus Christ.

56. In Exodus 23:25, the Bible says, you shall serve the LORD your God, and He will bless your bread and your

water, and I will take sickness away from among you. O God my Father, you are Jehovah Rapha, take away every sickness from my family, in the name of Jesus Christ.

57. In Exodus 23:25, the Bible says, you shall serve the LORD your God, and He will bless your bread and your water, and I will take sickness away from among you. O God my Father, you are Jehovah Rapha, take away every sickness from my household, in the name of Jesus Christ.

I cover my prayers in the blood of Jesus Christ. According to the Word of God, I have asked; I shall receive. I have knocked the door; it shall be opened unto me. I have sought; I shall find, in the name of Jesus Christ. It is written, "… Decree a thing, and it shall be established". As I have spoken in prayer, it shall be so. My prayers shall produce desired results. My prayers shall produce desired miracles. My prayers shall produce desired testimonies, in the name of Jesus Christ. Territorial spirit and power cannot hinder this prayer. Sins and flesh cannot hinder this prayer. It is done. It is sealed by the blood of Jesus Christ. It is delivered to me, in Jesus mighty name. Amen!

DAY TWO

PRAYER FOR DIVINE REVELATION

Passages To Read Before You Pray:

Amos 3:7, Job 12:22, Daniel 2:22, Psalm 25, 30, 19, 24

In the book of Job 22:28, the Scripture says when I decree a thing, it shall be established for me. I stand on this Scripture and decree. I have come into the presence of God today to plead my case. I enter through the gate of praise, into the sanctuary of heaven. I cover myself in the precious blood of Jesus Christ. I baptize myself in the fire of the Holy Ghost. I charge this atmosphere with the fire of God, and I take this neighborhood for the Lord. I arrest every principality and power, territorial spirit, and every throne and kingdom that is not of God. I cast you down and I command you never to lift yourself up against me, because I have the life of God in me.

In the name of Jesus Christ, I confess my sins today, and I ask you O Lord to forgive me on the basis of your mercy. With all my heart, I forgive those who have sinned against me; from the past through this moment. I release them from any form of guilt and shame, in the name of Jesus Christ. I hereby plead the blood of Jesus over any sins committed by my parents and ancestors. I cancel through the Blood of Jesus Christ, any satanic covenants, exchanges, vows or transactions, made over my life, body, soul, spirit, and circumstances, in the name of Jesus Christ. I cancel every legal right that the devil may have against me, by the blood of Jesus Christ. The accuser of the brethren will have nothing against me, as I come to the presence of God in prayer.

The devil cannot hinder or delay my prayer, because I know who I am. I am a child of the Kingdom. I am a king and priest of the Lord, redeemed from the hand of the devil by the blood of Jesus Christ. I walk in power. I walk in miracle. Proverbs 18:21 says, death and life are in the power of my tongue; I command the power in my tongue to manifest now. I command my tongue to become fire, to consume all the powers of darkness in the air, the land, the sea, and beneath the earth. I hereby raise Holy Ghost standard against the prince of the power of the air and all the hosts of darkness in the air. I raise Holy Ghost standard against the queen of the coasts and all the hosts of darkness on the land. I raise Holy Ghost standard against the marine kingdom and all the hosts of darkness in the sea. I raise Holy Ghost standard against the kingdom of hell and all the hosts of darkness beneath the earth. I shoot down all the networks of demons gathering to resist my prayers. I rebuke and bind all the controlling forces of darkness standing against my prayers.

I declare that all satanic thrones, altars, dominions, principalities, powers, rulers of darkness, queens of the coast, queens of heavens, household wickedness, spiritual hosts of wickedness and all satanic works, have no power or authority over my life. I declare that satanic harassment and intimidation have no effect on me.

Today, I receive divine strength to pray; I will not pray in vain. I will not pray amiss. My prayers will bring the desired results. I command the fountain of prayer to open now, and to flow into my life, I command the warring angels of God to descend and fight on my behalf. Every minute and every hour that I spend in prayer, will bring solution. Every prayer point will attract divine attention and divine intervention. I decree open heavens over my

prayers, and today, God of heaven and earth will attend to my case. My prayers today will shake the heavens and move the earth. Testimonies, miracles, healings, breakthroughs, and signs and wonders, will follow my prayers. At the end of this prayer session, my life will never be the same again.

PRAYER POINTS

1. O God my Father, thank you for being my God, my Father and my friend.
2. O God my Father, thank you for the privilege to know you and the power of the resurrection of Jesus Christ.
3. O God my Father, thank you for always being there for me and with me.
4. O God my Father, thank you for the great and mighty things that you are doing in my life.
5. O God my Father, thank you for your provision and protection over me and my household.
6. O God my Father, thank you for always answering my prayers.
7. I confess my sins before you today and I ask you to forgive me on the basis of your mercy, in the name of Jesus Christ.
8. Wash me clean today O Lord by the blood of Jesus Christ.
9. I cover myself and my household with the blood of Jesus Christ.
10. My prayers today will not go in vain; my prayers will produce the desired results in the name of Jesus Christ.
11. O God my Father, open my spiritual eyes that I may see what you want me to see, in the name of name of Jesus

Christ.

12. I stand on the Word of God. I receive grace to see beyond the natural into the supernatural, in the name of Jesus Christ.

13. I stand on the Word of God. I receive grace to see what God wants me to see concerning this particular situation in my life, in the name of Jesus Christ.

14. I stand on the Word of God. I receive grace to see what God wants me to see concerning this particular situation in my marriage, in the name of Jesus Christ.

15. I stand on the Word of God. I receive grace to see what God wants me to see concerning this particular situation in my business, in the name of Jesus Christ.

16. I stand on the Word of God. I receive grace to see what God wants me to see concerning this problem in my life, in the name of Jesus Christ.

17. I stand on the Word of God. I receive grace to see what God wants me to see concerning this particular person, in the name of Jesus Christ.

18. I stand on the Word of God. I receive grace to see what God wants me to see concerning the decision I am about to make, in the name of Jesus Christ.

19. I stand on the Word of God. I receive grace to see what God wants me to see concerning the step I should take in life, in the name of Jesus Christ.

20. I stand on the Word of God. I receive grace to see what God wants me to see concerning whether I should wait or move, in the name of Jesus Christ.

21. O God my Father, let anything blocking my spiritual vision be removed and destroyed now, in the name of Jesus Christ.

22. I stand on the Word of God. I receive grace to know the

mind of God concerning my life, in the name of Jesus Christ.

23. I stand on the Word of God. I receive grace to know the mind of God concerning my family, in the name of Jesus Christ.

24. I stand on the Word of God. I receive grace to know the mind of God concerning my marriage, in the name of Jesus Christ.

25. I stand on the Word of God. I receive grace to know the mind of God concerning my destiny, in the name of Jesus Christ.

26. I stand on the Word of God. I receive grace to know the mind of God concerning my future, in the name of Jesus Christ.

27. I stand on the Word of God. I receive grace to know the mind of God concerning my spouse, in the name of Jesus Christ.

28. I stand on the Word of God. I receive grace to know the mind of God concerning my children, in the name of Jesus Christ.

29. I stand on the Word of God. I receive grace to know the mind of God concerning my career, in the name of Jesus Christ.

30. I stand on the Word of God. I receive grace to know the mind of God concerning my ministry, in the name of Jesus Christ.

31. I stand on the Word of God. I receive grace to know the mind of God concerning my finances, in the name of Jesus Christ.

32. I stand on the Word of God. I receive grace to know the mind of God concerning my relocation, in the name of Jesus Christ.

33. Any power anywhere trying to keep me in the dark; I arrest you, bind and cast you down into the pit of hell. You will not prosper, in the name of Jesus Christ.
34. I stand on the Word of God. I reject spiritual blindness, in the name of Jesus Christ.
35. I stand on the Word of God. I reject confusion; I receive a sound mind and clear revelation, in the name of Jesus Christ.
36. By the authority and power in the name of Jesus Christ, I receive divine guidance in every area of life, in the name of Jesus Christ.
37. By the authority and power in the name of Jesus Christ, I receive divine guidance in any direction I follow; I will not miss my way, in the name of Jesus Christ.
38. By the authority and power in the name of Jesus Christ, I receive divine guidance in any path I take; I will not miss my way, in the name of Jesus Christ.
39. By the authority and power in the name of Jesus Christ, I receive divine guidance in any decision I make; I will not miss my way, in the name of Jesus Christ.
40. By the authority and power in the name of Jesus Christ, I receive divine guidance even before I open my mouth to speak, in the name of Jesus Christ.
41. By the authority and power in the name of Jesus Christ, I receive divine revelation concerning my future, in the name of Jesus Christ.
42. By the authority and power in the name of Jesus Christ, I receive divine revelation concerning my destiny, in the name of Jesus Christ.
43. By the authority and power in the name of Jesus Christ, I receive divine revelation concerning the next step I should take in life, in the name of Jesus Christ.

44. By the authority and power in the name of Jesus Christ, I receive divine revelation concerning my questions and concerns, in the name of Jesus Christ.
45. By the authority and power in the name of Jesus Christ, I receive divine revelation concerning God's plans and agenda for my life, in the name of Jesus Christ.
46. By the authority and power in the name of Jesus Christ, I receive divine revelation concerning what God wants me to do in life, in the name of Jesus Christ.
47. By the authority and power in the name of Jesus Christ, I receive divine revelation concerning what I am praying for, in the name of Jesus Christ.
48. By the authority and power in the name of Jesus Christ, I receive divine revelation concerning my purpose in life, in the name of Jesus Christ.
49. By the authority and power in the name of Jesus Christ, I receive answers to my difficult questions, in the name of Jesus Christ.
50. By the authority and power in the name of Jesus Christ, I receive answers to my prayers, in the name of Jesus Christ.

I cover my prayers in the blood of Jesus Christ. According to the Word of God, I have asked; I shall receive. I have knocked the door; it shall be opened unto me. I have sought; I shall find, in the name of Jesus Christ. It is written, "… Decree a thing, and it shall be established". As I have spoken in prayer, it shall be so. My prayers shall produce desired results. My prayers shall produce desired miracles. My prayers shall produce desired testimonies, in the name of Jesus Christ. Territorial spirit and power cannot hinder this prayer. Sins and flesh cannot hinder this prayer. It is done. It is sealed by the blood of Jesus Christ. It is delivered to me, in Jesus mighty name. Amen!

DAY THREE

PRAYER TO RECEIVE INSTANT MIRACLE

Passages To Read Before You Pray:
2 Kings 7:1-20, Mark 5:25-34, Psalms 103, 86, 30, 24

In the book of Job 22:28, the Scripture says when I decree a thing, it shall be established for me. I stand on this Scripture and decree. I have come today to fellowship with my heavenly Father, and make my requests and needs known unto Him. I cannot be hindered nor delayed because I know who I am in the Lord. I am a child of the Kingdom, born of the Spirit, redeemed by the blood of Jesus Christ. I walk in authority, living life without any apology because the power and authority has been given to me according to the Word of God in the book of Luke 9:1.

As I have come to pray today and to fellowship with my heavenly Father, I cover myself in the blood of Jesus Christ, and I put on the whole armor of God. I hereby come against every Prince of Persia that wants to hinder my prayer, I arrest you by the power in the blood of Jesus Christ, and I bind you and cast you down into the pit of hell.

I come against principalities and powers that wrestle with me and my prayers, I arrest you today by the power in the name of Jesus Christ, and I bind you and cast down into the pit of hell. I come against the rulers of the darkness of this world, against spiritual wickedness in high places, I arrest you all by the power in the name of Jesus Christ, and I bind you and cast you down into the pit of hell. I come against weakness and weariness, I arrest you today by the power in the name of Jesus Christ, and I

bind you and cast you out of my life. I come against wondering spirit and distractions, I arrest you today by the power in the name of Jesus Christ, and I bind you and cast you out of my life.

Today I receive the anointing to pray and get results, my prayers cannot be hindered nor delayed because Jesus is my Lord, I will pray today and get the desired results, I decree open heavens upon my prayers. I baptize myself in the fire of the Holy Ghost; therefore I have become too hot for the enemy to handle. My prayers today will attract divine intervention to every situation in my life; signs and wonders will follow my prayers today, testimonies will follow my prayers today and the name of God alone will be glorified, in Jesus name. Amen!

PRAYER POINTS

1. O God my Father, thank you for being my God, my Father and my friend.
2. O God my Father, thank you for the privilege to know you and the power of the resurrection of Jesus Christ.
3. O God my Father, thank you for always being there for me and with me.
4. O God my Father, thank you for the great and mighty things that you are doing in my life.
5. O God my Father, thank you for your provision and protection over me and my household.
6. O God my Father, thank you for always answering my prayers.
7. I confess my sins before you today and I ask you to forgive me on the basis of your mercy, in the name of Jesus Christ.

8. Wash me clean today O Lord by the blood of Jesus Christ.
9. I cover myself and my household with the blood of Jesus Christ.
10. My prayers today will not go in vain; my prayers will produce the desired results, in the name of Jesus Christ.
11. O God my Father, let every decision of the enemy against me be overturned, in the name of Jesus Christ.
12. O God my Father, let every plan of the enemy to rob me of my joy be overturned, in the name of Jesus Christ.
13. O God my Father, let every plan of the enemy to rob me of my testimonies be overturned, in the name of Jesus Christ.
14. O God my Father, let it be my turn to testify, in the name of Jesus Christ.
15. O God my Father, let anything in my life robbing me of my testimonies, be destroyed by the fire of God.
16. O God my Father, release into my life today overnight miracles, in the name of Jesus Christ.
17. By this time tomorrow, I will surely have my testimonies, in the name of Jesus Christ.
18. By this time tomorrow, I will surely have my miracles, in the name of Jesus Christ.
19. By this time tomorrow, I will surely have answers to my prayers, in the name of Jesus Christ.
20. By this time tomorrow, I will have abundance in my life instead of lack, in the name of Jesus Christ.
21. By this time tomorrow, I will have testimonies concerning the promotions that I have been praying for, in the name of Jesus Christ.

22. By this time tomorrow, I will have testimonies concerning the breakthroughs that I am praying for, in the name of Jesus Christ.

23. By this time tomorrow, I will have testimonies concerning my business or career that I am praying for, in the name of Jesus Christ.

24. By this time tomorrow, I will have surplus in every area of my life.

25. By this time tomorrow, I will celebrate my victory over the plan of the enemy.

26. Every hindrance to my breakthrough is removed today by the fire of God.

27. Every obstacle to my progress is removed today by the fire of God.

28. O God my Father, by this time tomorrow, you will give me every reason to testify.

29. O God my Father, it is my turn to testify, do something in my life today that will bring a complete turn-around.

30. O God my Father, it is my turn to testify, let there be a total transformation in every area of my life.

31. O God my Father, it is my turn to testify, you are permitted to move my life forward by force.

32. O God my Father, it is my turn to testify, you are permitted to change whatever needs to be changed in my life.

33. O God my Father, it is my turn to testify, you are permitted to destroy anything in my life that is holding me back from fulfilling purpose, in the name of Jesus Christ.

34. By this time tomorrow, there must be a positive change in every area of my life to the glory of God.

35. O God my Father, it is my turn to testify, let there be a total restoration in every area of my life, in the name of Jesus Christ.

I cover my prayers in the blood of Jesus Christ. According to the Word of God, I have asked; I shall receive. I have knocked the door; it shall be opened unto me. I have sought; I shall find, in the name of Jesus Christ. It is written, "… Decree a thing, and it shall be established". As I have spoken in prayer, it shall be so. My prayers shall produce desired results. My prayers shall produce desired miracles. My prayers shall produce desired testimonies, in the name of Jesus Christ. Territorial spirit and power cannot hinder this prayer. Sins and flesh cannot hinder this prayer. It is done. It is sealed by the blood of Jesus Christ. It is delivered to me, in Jesus mighty name. Amen!

DAY FOUR

DELIVERANCE FROM THE SPIRIT OF ALMOST THERE

Passages To Read Before You Pray:
Obadiah 1:17, Isaiah 10:27, Galatians 3:13,
Psalms 35, 55, 10, 57, 83

In the book of Job 22:28, the Scripture says when I decree a thing, it shall be established for me. I stand on this Scripture and decree. I claim my right as a child of the Kingdom, I cover myself in the blood of Jesus Christ, I cover my household and everything concerning me in the blood of Jesus Christ. I hereby charge this atmosphere by the blood of Jesus Christ and by the fire of the Holy Ghost. I command fresh fire of God to rest upon me now as in the day of Pentecost, let fresh anointing and new oil be released upon me now as I pray. I receive power and authority over the power and the kingdom of darkness, to root out and to pull down, to destroy and to throw down, to build and to plant; whatever I decree in this prayer shall be established; whatever I bind today shall be bound in heaven and whatever I loose today shall be loosed in heaven as it is written in the word of God. Let fresh fire of God be released on my prayer altar and my prayer life now, prince of Persia cannot hinder my prayer, territorial spirit of my neighborhood cannot hinder my prayer, household wickedness cannot hinder my prayer.

I can see my prayer attracting divine intervention. This is the day that the Lord has made, I will rejoice and be glad in it. This is the day that the Lord has chosen to set me free from any form of bondage and break any form of curses upon my life; this is the day that I will receive a total and complete deliverance in every area of my life, today shall mark the beginning of a new thing in my life.

I am a child of God, born of the Spirit, redeemed by the blood of the Lamb. It is written concerning me that power and authority is given unto me over all devils and to cure diseases, I hereby take authority over any form of curses upon my life, be it ancestral, be it generational, be it demon-inflicted or self-inflicted; I command all curses upon my life to break now by the authority in the name of Jesus Christ. The Bible says, where the word of a king is, there is power; today I speak as a king with the authority and power of the King of kings, and I command every other power to bow in the name of Jesus Christ. I render any power behind any curse upon my life useless and ineffective; I overcome any form of distraction, spiritual laziness and slumber, before the end of this prayer session my testimonies shall manifest without delay by the power in the name of Jesus Christ. Amen!

PRAYER POINTS

1. O God my Father, thank you for being my God, my Father and my friend.
2. O God my Father, thank you for the privilege to know you and the power of the resurrection of Jesus Christ.
3. O God my Father, thank you for always being there for me and with me.
4. O God my Father, thank you for the great and mighty things that you are doing in my life.
5. O God my Father, thank you for your provision and protection over me and my household.

6. O God my Father, thank you for always answering my prayers.
7. I confess my sins before you today and I ask you to forgive me on the basis of your mercy, in the name of Jesus Christ.
8. Wash me clean today O Lord by the blood of Jesus Christ.
9. I cover myself and my household with the blood of Jesus Christ.
10. My prayers today will not go in vain; my prayers will produce the desired results in the name of Jesus Christ.
11. Seeing it but not receiving it is not for me, I therefore see and receive the blessings of the Lord over my life by the power in the name of Jesus Christ.
12. Seeing it but not receiving it is not for me, I therefore see and receive the blessings of the Lord over my family by the power in the name of Jesus Christ.
13. Seeing it but not receiving it is not for me, I therefore see and receive the blessings of the Lord over my marriage by the power in the name of Jesus Christ.
14. Seeing it but not receiving it is not for me, I therefore see and receive the blessings of the Lord concerning my business by the power in the name of Jesus Christ.
15. Seeing it but not receiving it is not for me, I therefore see and receive the blessings of the Lord concerning my finances by the power in the name of Jesus Christ.
16. Seeing it but not receiving it is not for me, I therefore see and receive the blessings of the Lord concerning my future by the power in the name of Jesus Christ.
17. Seeing it but not receiving it is not for me, I therefore see and receive the blessings of the Lord concerning my destiny by the power in the name of Jesus Christ.

18. Seeing it but not receiving it is not for me, I therefore see and receive the blessings of the Lord concerning my goals and dreams by the power in the name of Jesus Christ.

19. Seeing it but not receiving it is not for me, I therefore see and receive the blessings of the Lord concerning my spouse by the power in the name of Jesus Christ.

20. Seeing it but not receiving it is not for me, I therefore see and receive the blessings of the Lord concerning my children by the power in the name of Jesus Christ.

21. I cut off any connection which my life may have with the spirit of last minute failure, in the name of Jesus Christ.

22. I cut off any connection which my life may have with the spirit of last minute failure from my father's lineage by the fire of God, in the name of Jesus Christ.

23. I cut off any connection which my life may have with the spirit of last minute failure from my mother's lineage by the fire of God, in the name of Jesus Christ.

24. I destroy every agent of failure assigned to work against me by the fire of God, in the name of Jesus Christ

25. I destroy every agent of failure that has been working in my bloodline from generation to generation by the fire of God, in the name of Jesus Christ.

26. I destroy every agent of failure assigned to work against my spouse by the fire of God, in the name of Jesus Christ.

27. I destroy every agent of failure assigned to work against my children by the fire of God, in the name of Jesus Christ.

28. I destroy every agent of failure assigned to work against my future generations by the fire of God, in the name of Jesus Christ.

29. O God my Father, let the satanic mandate calculated to bring chaos at the edge of my breakthrough be nullified by the power in the name of Jesus Christ.

30. O God my Father, let the satanic mandate calculated to bring chaos at the edge of my success be nullified by the power in the name of Jesus Christ.

31. O God my Father, let the satanic mandate calculated to bring chaos at the edge of my miracle be nullified by the power in the name of Jesus Christ.

32. O God my Father, let the satanic mandate calculated to bring chaos at the edge of my testimony be nullified by the power in the name of Jesus Christ.

33. O God my Father, arise and destroy every challenge at the edge of my testimony, in the name of Jesus Christ.

34. O God my Father, arise and destroy every challenge at the edge of my miracle, in the name of Jesus Christ.

35. O God my Father, arise and destroy every challenge at the edge of my breakthrough, in the name of Jesus Christ.

36. O God my Father, arise and destroy every challenge at the point of my promotion, in the name of Jesus Christ.

37. O God my Father, arise and destroy every challenge at the edge of my success, in the name of Jesus Christ.

38. O God my Father, arise and destroy every challenge at the edge of my financial freedom, in the name of Jesus Christ.

39. O God my Father, arise and destroy every challenge at the edge of my business success, in the name of Jesus Christ.

40. O God my Father, arise and destroy every challenge at the edge of my ministerial success, in the name of Jesus Christ.

I cover my prayers in the blood of Jesus Christ. According to the Word of God, I have asked; I shall receive. I have knocked the door; it shall be opened unto me. I have sought; I shall find, in the name of Jesus Christ. It is written, "… Decree a thing, and it shall be established". As I have spoken in prayer, it shall be so. My prayers shall produce desired results. My prayers shall produce desired miracles. My prayers shall produce desired testimonies, in the name of Jesus Christ. Territorial spirit and power cannot hinder this prayer. Sins and flesh cannot hinder this prayer. It is done. It is sealed by the blood of Jesus Christ. It is delivered to me, in Jesus mighty name. Amen!

DAY FIVE

ARISE O LORD, & SHOWCASE YOUR POWER

Passages To Read Before You Pray:
Isaiah 43:18-19, 2 Kings 2:1-18, John 11:1-48,
Psalms 46, 19, 126

In the book of Job 22:28, the Scripture says when I decree a thing, it shall be established for me. I stand on this Scripture and decree. I have come today to fellowship with my heavenly Father, and make my requests and needs known unto Him. I cannot be hindered nor delayed because I know who I am in the Lord. I am a child of the Kingdom, born of the Spirit, redeemed by the blood of Jesus Christ. I walk in authority, living life without any apology because the power and authority has been given to me according to the Word of God in the book of Luke 9:1.

As I have come to pray today and to fellowship with my heavenly Father, I cover myself in the blood of Jesus Christ, and I put on the whole armor of God. I hereby come against every Prince of Persia that wants to hinder my prayer, I arrest you by the power in the blood of Jesus Christ, and I bind you and cast you down into the pit of hell.

I come against principalities and powers that wrestle with me and my prayers, I arrest you today by the power in the name of Jesus Christ, and I bind you and cast down into the pit of hell. I come against the rulers of the darkness of this world, against spiritual wickedness in high places, I arrest you all by the power in the name of Jesus Christ, and I bind you and cast you down into the pit of hell. I come against weakness and weariness, I

arrest you today by the power in the name of Jesus Christ, and I bind you and cast you out of my life. I come against wondering spirit and distractions, I arrest you today by the power in the name of Jesus Christ, and I bind you and cast you out of my life.

Today I receive the anointing to pray and get results, my prayers cannot be hindered nor delayed because Jesus is my Lord, I will pray today and get the desired results, I decree open heavens upon my prayers. I baptize myself in the fire of the Holy Ghost; therefore I have become too hot for the enemy to handle. My prayers today will attract divine intervention to every situation in my life; signs and wonders will follow my prayers today, testimonies will follow my prayers today and the name of God alone will be glorified, in Jesus name. Amen!

PRAYER POINTS

1. O God my Father, thank you for being my God, my Father and my friend.
2. O God my Father, thank you for the privilege to know you and the power of the resurrection of Jesus Christ.
3. O God my Father, thank you for always being there for me and with me.
4. O God my Father, thank you for the great and mighty things that you are doing in my life.
5. O God my Father, thank you for your provision and protection over me and my household.
6. O God my Father, thank you for always answering my prayers.

7. I confess my sins before you today and I ask you to forgive me on the basis of your mercy, in the name of Jesus Christ.

8. Wash me clean today O Lord by the blood of Jesus Christ.

9. I cover myself and my household with the blood of Jesus Christ.

10. My prayers today will not go in vain; my prayers will produce the desired results in the name of Jesus Christ.

11. In the presence of those who are waiting to mock me, O God my Father, demonstrate your power that they may know that you are my God, in the name of Jesus Christ.

12. In the presence of those who are waiting to celebrate my failure, O God my Father, grant me an immeasurable success that they may know you are my God, in the name of Jesus Christ.

13. In the presence of those who are waiting to see what will become of me, O God my Father, demonstrate your power that they may know you are my God, in the name of Jesus Christ.

14. In the presence of those who are waiting to mock the outcome of my prayers, O God my Father, answer my prayer by fire that they may know you are my God, in the name of Jesus Christ.

15. O God my Father, in the presence of those who are waiting to see what you can do for me, demonstrate your power that they may know that you can do all things, in the name of Jesus Christ.

16. O God my Father, in the presence of those who are waiting to see me fall, demonstrate your power that they may know that you are my God, in the name of Jesus Christ.

17. O God my Father, in the presence of those who are waiting to point evil fingers at me, demonstrate your power that they may know you are my God, in the name of Jesus Christ.
18. My helpers, wherever you are, I command you to come forth, in the name of Jesus Christ.
19. My glory, wherever you are, I command you to come forth, in the name of Jesus Christ.
20. My financial freedom, wherever you are, I command you to come forth, in the name of Jesus Christ.
21. My miracles, wherever you are, I command you to come forth, in the name of Jesus Christ.
22. My blessings, wherever you are, I command you to come forth, in the name of Jesus Christ.
23. My financial breakthrough, wherever you are, I command you to come forth, in the name of Jesus Christ.
24. My success, wherever you are, I command you to come forth, in the name of Jesus Christ.
25. People that will show me the way, wherever you are, I command you to come forth, in the name of Jesus Christ.
26. People that will lead me to the top, wherever you are, I command you to come forth, in the name of Jesus Christ.
27. People that God sent to support me, wherever you are, I command you to come forth, in the name of Jesus Christ.
28. People that will show me how to make it, wherever you are, I command you to come forth, in the name of Jesus Christ.
29. People that will contribute to my success, wherever you are, I command you to come forth, in the name of Jesus Christ.

30. People that will show me how to get to the next level, wherever you are, I command you to come forth, in the name of Jesus Christ.
31. People that will connect me to those that will help me, wherever you are, I command you to come forth, in the name of Jesus Christ.
32. O God my Father, I am tired of being the same, let transformation begin to happen in every area of my life, in the name of Jesus Christ.
33. O God my Father, I am tired of being the same, let the new things begin to happen in every area of my life, in the name of Jesus Christ.
34. O God my Father, I am tired of being the same, begin to showcase your power in my life, in the name of Jesus Christ.
35. O God my Father, I am tired of being the same, let extraordinary things begin to happen in my life, in the name of Jesus Christ.
36. O God my Father, I am tired of being the same, let there be supernatural breakthrough in every area of my life, in the name of Jesus Christ.
37. O God my Father, I am tired of being the same, take me from where I am to where you want me to be, in the name of Jesus Christ.
38. O God my Father, I am tired of being the same, catapult me into greatness, in the name of Jesus Christ.
39. O God my Father, I am tired of being the same, catapult me into double promotion, in the name of Jesus Christ.
40. O God my Father, I am tired of being the same, take me to the next level of your power, in the name of Jesus Christ.

41. O God my Father, I am tired of being the same, take me to the next level of your glory, in the name of Jesus Christ.

42. O God my Father, I am tired of being the same, take me to the next level of prosperity, in the name of Jesus Christ.

43. O God my Father, I am tired of being the same, take me to the place of fulfillment, in the name of Jesus Christ.

44. O God my Father, I am tired of being the same, take me to the land that is flowing with milk and honey, in the name of Jesus Christ.

45. O God my Father, I am tired of being the same, transfer me from the valley to the mountain top, in the name of Jesus Christ.

46. O God my Father, I am tired of being the same, let the great and mighty things that you promise begin to happen in my life, in the name of Jesus Christ.

47. O God my Father, I am tired of being the same, give me reasons to sing a new song, in the name of Jesus Christ.

48. O God my Father, I am tired of being the same, give me reasons to dance a new dance, in the name of Jesus Christ.

49. O God my Father, I am tired of being the same, let your power bring the best out of me, in the name of Jesus Christ.

50. O God my Father, I'm tired of being the same, give me reasons to laugh a new laugh, in the name of Jesus Christ.

I cover my prayers in the blood of Jesus Christ. According to the Word of God, I have asked; I shall receive. I have knocked the door; it shall be opened unto me. I have sought; I shall find, in the name of Jesus Christ. It is written, "… Decree a thing, and it shall be established". As I have spoken in prayer, it shall be so. My prayers shall produce desired results. My prayers shall produce desired miracles. My prayers shall produce desired testimonies, in the name of Jesus Christ. Territorial spirit and power cannot hinder this prayer. Sins and flesh cannot hinder this prayer. It is done. It is sealed by the blood of Jesus Christ. It is delivered to me, in Jesus mighty name. Amen!

DAY SIX

PRAYER FOR SIGNS AND WONDERS

Passages To Read Before You Pray:
Mark 5:25-34, Mark 10:46-52, Isaiah 43:19,
Genesis 8:15-22, Joel 2:21-27, Habakkuk 1:5

In the book of Job 22:28, the Scripture says when I decree a thing, it shall be established for me. I stand on this Scripture and decree. I have come into the presence of God today to plead my case. I enter through the gate of praise into the sanctuary of heaven. I cover myself in the precious blood of Jesus Christ. I baptize myself in the fire of the Holy Ghost. I charge this atmosphere with the fire of God, and I take this neighborhood for the Lord. I arrest every principality and power, territorial spirit, and every throne and kingdom that is not of God. I cast you down and I command you never to lift yourself up against me, because I have the life of God in me.

In the name of Jesus Christ, I confess my sins today, and I ask you O Lord to forgive me on the basis of your mercy. With all my heart, I forgive those who have sinned against me from the past through this moment. I release them from any form of guilt and shame, in the name of Jesus Christ. I hereby plead the blood of Jesus over any sins committed by my parents and ancestors. I cancel through the Blood of Jesus Christ, any satanic covenants, exchanges, vows or transactions made over my life, body, soul, spirit, and circumstances, in the name of Jesus Christ. I cancel every legal right that the devil may have against me, by the blood of Jesus Christ. The accuser of the brethren will have nothing against me as I come to the presence of God in prayer.

The devil cannot hinder or delay my prayer, because I know who I am. I am a child of the Kingdom; I am a king and priest of the Lord, redeemed from the hand of the devil by the blood of Jesus Christ. I declare that all satanic thrones, altars, dominions, principalities, powers, rulers of darkness, queen of the coast, queen of heavens, household wickedness, spiritual hosts of wickedness and all satanic works, have no power or authority over my life. I declare that satanic harassment and intimidation have no effect on me.

Today I receive divine strength to pray; I will not pray in vain. I will not pray amiss. My prayers will bring the desired results. I command the fountain of prayer to open now, and flow into my life, I command the warring angels of God to descend and fight on my behalf. Every minute and every hour that I spend in prayer will bring solution. Every prayer point will attract divine attention and divine intervention. I decree open heavens over my prayers, and today, God of heaven and earth will attend to my case. My prayers today will shake the heavens and move the earth; testimonies, miracles, healing, breakthrough, signs and wonders will follow my prayers. At the end of this prayer session, my life will never be the same again.

PRAYER POINTS

1. O God my Father, thank you for being my God, my Father and my friend.
2. O God my Father, thank you for the privilege to know you and the power of the resurrection of Jesus Christ.
3. O God my Father, thank you for always being there for me and with me.

4. O God my Father, thank you for the great and mighty things that you are doing in my life.
5. O God my Father, thank you for your provision and protection over me and my household.
6. O God my Father, thank you for always answering my prayers.
7. I confess my sins before you today and I ask you to forgive me on the basis of your mercy, in the name of Jesus Christ.
8. Wash me clean today O Lord by the blood of Jesus Christ.
9. I cover myself and my household with the blood of Jesus Christ.
10. My prayers today will not go in vain; my prayers will produce the desired results in the name of Jesus Christ.
11. By the authority and power in the blood of Jesus Christ, I decree that my dream will not hold me back this year; my dream will not hold me captive, and I will not be defeated in the dream, in the name of Jesus Christ.
12. I use the blood of Jesus Christ to silence anybody anywhere prophesying evil into my life, in the name of Jesus Christ.
13. All outstanding testimonies of my prayer, I command you to manifest speedily now, in the name of Jesus Christ.
14. By the authority and power in the blood of Jesus Christ, I nullify every evil covenant of little mistakes that hinders a man not to fulfill his destiny. You have no power over my life, in the name of Jesus Christ.
15. By the authority and power in the blood of Jesus Christ, I arrest any power anywhere postponing the day of joy

and testimony in my life. I command you to loose your hold over my life, in the name of Jesus Christ.

16. I stand on the Word of God. I decree that sin will not hinder me on my day of divine visitation. I shall be rightly located to receive my blessings, in the name of Jesus Christ.

17. O God my Father, according to your Word; perfect everything that concerns me, in the name of Jesus Christ.

18. I stand on the Word of God. I declare that I shall not operate below or outside my purpose; and I will not fall out of grace, in the name of Jesus Christ.

19. O God my Father, complete me today in every area that people see me as incomplete, and in every area that I lack good things, in the name of Jesus Christ.

20. Every spirit of impossibility in my life, O God of Elijah scatter them by fire today, in the name of Jesus Christ.

21. O God my Father, reveal every ungodly relationship in my life; scatter them by the fire of God, in the name of Jesus Christ.

22. I separate myself from every unfriendly friend assigned to hinder my progress, in the name of Jesus Christ.

23. I release the fire of God to scatter every evil gathering against me, in the name of Jesus Christ.

24. In the name that is above all other names, I decree abundance of blessings upon my life today, in the name of Jesus Christ.

25. I prophesy abundance of goodness into my future now, in the name of Jesus Christ.

26. O God my Father, let the spirit of prophet and prophecy be released upon me today, and make me prosper in all areas of my life, in the name of Jesus Christ.

27. O God my Father, beautify my life beyond my imagination this year, and let people see your wonder working hand in my situation, in the name of Jesus Christ.

28. O God my Father, arise and scatter every conspiracy against my destiny, in the name of Jesus Christ.

29. O God my Father, arise and remove every hindrance to my rising and shining this year, in the name of Jesus Christ.

30. In spite of the efforts and temptations of the enemy, I shall surely reach and achieve my life goals, in the name of Jesus Christ.

31. O God my Father, let any power anywhere assigned to distract me this year be disappointed, in the name of Jesus Christ.

32. I stand on the Word of God. I decree that I shall not operate below or outside my destiny; and my destiny will not suffer affliction, in the name of Jesus Christ.

33. O God my Father, order my steps to be in an environment where I will discover and fulfill my dreams, in the name of Jesus Christ.

34. O God my Father, make me wiser than my enemies this year, and give me more understanding than my competitors, in the name of Jesus Christ.

35. O God my Father, let mercy prevail over judgment for me. In your wrath remember mercy, in the name of Jesus Christ.

36. O God my Father, answer my prayers today, and give me reasons to testify and celebrate, in the name of Jesus Christ.

37. Because my foundation is in Christ Jesus, no evil wind or storm will blow me away. I am grounded in the Lord, in the name of Jesus Christ.

38. O God of perfect timing; appear in my situation now, in the name of Jesus Christ.

39. O God my Father, let my life manifest your glory so that the whole world will know that I serve a Mighty God, in the name of Jesus Christ.

40. Spirit of the living God, re-arrange my life today and take me to my favor. Bring me to my helpers and bring my helpers to me now, in the name that is above all names; in the name of Jesus Christ.

41. I stand on the Word of God. I declare that I am redeemed from the curse of the law, and I am no more under bondage. I shall continue to prosper from now; in health and in wealth, even as my soul prospers, in the name of Jesus Christ.

42. I stand on the Word of God. I decree that mercy of God will meet with grace of God upon my life today, and my breakthrough will come forth this season, in the name of Jesus Christ.

43. O God my Father, let the Spirit of greatness locate me now and make me great, in the name of Jesus Christ.

44. I am designed for greatness! O Great God, let my greatness manifest now, in the name of Jesus Christ.

45. I stand on the Word of God. I decree that in every day and night of this year, I will go greater than before until I become very great in life, in the name of Jesus Christ.

46. I stand on the Word of God. I decree that I shall not fail this season, in the name of Jesus Christ.

47. I command every hindrance on my path to success to be consumed now, by the fire of the Most High God, in the name of Jesus Christ.
48. I stand on the Word of God. I decree that this year I will prosper physically, spiritually and financially, in the name of Jesus Christ.
49. O God my Father, by the reason of the anointing, fill my mouth with laughter and my tongues with songs of joy; today and forever, in the name of Jesus Christ.
50. O God my Father, let those who see me see your goodness and mighty works in my life, and say among themselves that God has done great things for him/her, in the name of Jesus Christ.
51. Spirit of deliverance come upon me now, in the name Jesus. I loose myself from all afflictions, in the mighty name of Jesus Christ.
52. By the authority in the blood of Jesus Christ, I decree that affliction shall not rise again in my life; affliction shall not rise in my family; all the rest of my days, no one will cause me trouble again, in the name of Jesus Christ.
53. I receive an excellent spirit upon my life today that will make me excel and get excellent results on all things that I set my hands to do, in the name of Jesus Christ.
54. All foul spirits that confuse man to do the wrong things at a wrong time, I rebuke you in my life today, in the name of Jesus Christ.
55. I stand on the Word of God. I declare that there is no room for foul spirits in my domain, in the name of Jesus Christ.

56. Holy Spirit of God, help me to give my best at the right time that will provoke uncommon blessings for me this season, in the name of Jesus Christ.

57. Because I follow the Lord, throughout this year good things will happen to me; good things will happen to my family; good things will happen to my city, in the name of Jesus Christ.

58. I decree in the name that is above all names that the power of the Most High God that turned scarcity to surplus within 24hours, in the land of Samaria, will turn around every area of my life that is lacking good things. And goodness will overflow in my life from today, in the name of Jesus Christ.

59. God of mercy and compassion, give me divine assistance today; a divine assistance that delivers 24hour miracles, in the name of Jesus Christ.

60. O God my Father, give me divine assistance on everything I set my heart to do, or lay my hands upon, that I may achieve my goals and fulfill my dreams, in the name of Jesus Christ.

61. Because I believe in the living God, through me, my family will be blessed; through me, the nations of the earth will be blessed, in the name of Jesus Christ.

62. By the power in the blood of Jesus, every evil covenant upon my life, either in my past, in present, or in my future, is broken today by the precious blood of Jesus Christ, in the name of Jesus Christ.

63. In all the remaining parts of this year, disaster will not come near me; it will not come near any of my family, in the name of Jesus Christ.

64. O God my Father, I have started this year strong. I receive the grace of God to finish strong, in the name of Jesus Christ.

65. O God my Father, let every conspiracy against me, or against any of my loved ones, be scattered by the fire of God, in the name of Jesus Christ.

66. Throughout the rest of this year, anything that will bring shame or disappointment will not be my portion. It will not happen in my family, in the name of Jesus Christ.

67. By the authority in the blood of Jesus Christ, I decree today that the land will yield its best fruits for me. The sun will bring forth its best for me, and the moon will yield its finest for me this year, in the name of Jesus Christ.

68. O God my Father, grant me mercy from Zion today. Where my eyes cannot reach, let your mercy speak for me, in the name of Jesus Christ.

69. Every evil tongue that planned to rise against me at the edge of my breakthrough, I silence you permanently, in the name of Jesus Christ.

70. O God my Father, let my fallen glory be restored and begin to shine forever and ever, in the name of Jesus Christ.

71. I stand on the Word of God. I declare that my life will not cause pain to my family; I will not be a disappointment to my loved ones, in the name of Jesus Christ.

72. I receive double blessings from God this season; I receive double favor, and I receive double anointing, in the name of Jesus Christ.

73. I declare, it does not matter how long I have struggled, or how long I have prayed for change to come, today I

decree a turn-around, and my prayer shall produce the desired results, in the name of Jesus Christ.

74. O God my Father, give me grace to recognize the opportunity that will take me to where I am destined to go in life, in the name of Jesus Christ.

75. I receive a direct Word from the Lord today; for instruction, correction and direction, in the name of Jesus Christ.

76. O God my Father, grant me uncommon favor this year and let there be a tremendous turn-around in my finances, in the name of Jesus Christ.

77. In the mighty name of Jesus, I will not suffer loss in any area of my life this year; I will not be a victim of any kind, and none of my family members will be a victim this year, in the name of Jesus Christ.

78. O God my Father, in the multitude of your tender mercies and loving kindness, blot out my transgressions and my family's transgressions today; so that past mistakes will cease to affect my life and my family, in the name of Jesus Christ.

79. O God my Father, release unto me the power to exercise spiritual authority and intellectual authority; power to exercise financial authority to flourish this year, in the name of Jesus Christ.

80. I stand on the Word of God. I decree that peace like a river flows into my troubled mind; the peace of Christ fills my heart and soul from this day; henceforth, in the name of Jesus Christ.

I cover my prayers in the blood of Jesus Christ. According to the Word of God, I have asked, I shall receive. I have knocked the door; it shall be opened unto me. I have sought, I shall find, in the name of Jesus Christ. It is written, "… Decree a thing, and it shall be established". As I have spoken in prayer, it shall be so. My prayers shall produce desire results. My prayers shall produce desired miracles. My prayers shall produce desired testimonies, in the name of Jesus Christ. Territorial spirit and power cannot hinder this prayer. Sins and flesh cannot hinder this prayer. It is done. It is sealed by the blood of Jesus Christ. It is delivered to me, in Jesus might name. Amen!

DAY SEVEN

PRAY AS A LAWFUL OWNER
OF ALL THINGS

Passages To Read Before You Pray:

Hebrews 1:2, Isaiah 45:2-3, Genesis 1:26,
Psalms 8, 86, 107

In the book of Job 22:28, the Scripture says when I decree a thing, it shall be established for me. I stand on this Scripture and decree. I have come into the presence of God today to plead my case. I enter through the gate of praise into the sanctuary of heaven. I cover myself in the precious blood of Jesus Christ. I baptize myself in the fire of the Holy Ghost. I charge this atmosphere with the fire of God, and I take this neighborhood for the Lord. I arrest every principality and power, territorial spirit, and every throne and kingdom that is not of God. I cast you down and I command you never to lift yourself up against me, because I have the life of God in me.

In the name of Jesus Christ, I confess my sins today, and I ask you O Lord to forgive me on the basis of your mercy. With all my heart, I forgive those who have sinned against me from the past through this moment. I release them from any form of guilt and shame, in the name of Jesus Christ. I hereby plead the blood of Jesus over any sins committed by my parents and ancestors. I cancel through the Blood of Jesus Christ, any satanic covenants, exchanges, vows or transactions made over my life, body, soul, spirit, and circumstances, in the name of Jesus Christ. I cancel every legal right that the devil may have against me, by the blood of Jesus Christ. The accuser of the brethren will have nothing against me as I come to the presence of God in prayer.

The devil cannot hinder or delay my prayer, because I know who I am. I am a child of the Kingdom; I am a king and priest of the Lord, redeemed from the hand of the devil by the blood of Jesus Christ. I declare that all satanic thrones, altars, dominions, principalities, powers, rulers of darkness, queen of the coast, queen of heavens, household wickedness, spiritual hosts of wickedness and all satanic works, have no power or authority over my life. I declare that satanic harassment and intimidation have no effect on me.

Today I receive divine strength to pray; I will not pray in vain. I will not pray amiss. My prayers will bring the desired results. I command the fountain of prayer to open now, and flow into my life, I command the warring angels of God to descend and fight on my behalf. Every minute and every hour that I spend in prayer will bring solution. Every prayer point will attract divine attention and divine intervention. I decree open heavens over my prayers, and today, God of heaven and earth will attend to my case. My prayers today will shake the heavens and move the earth; testimonies, miracles, healing, breakthrough, signs and wonders will follow my prayers. At the end of this prayer session, my life will never be the same again.

PRAYER POINTS

1. O God my Father, thank you for being my God, my Father and my friend.
2. O God my Father, thank you for the privilege to know you and the power of the resurrection of Jesus Christ.
3. O God my Father, thank you for always being there for me and with me.

4. O God my Father, thank you for the great and mighty things that you are doing in my life.
5. O God my Father, thank you for your provision and protection over me and my household.
6. O God my Father, thank you for always answering my prayers.
7. I confess my sins before you today and I ask you to forgive me on the basis of your mercy, in the name of Jesus Christ.
8. Wash me clean today O Lord by the blood of Jesus Christ.
9. I cover myself and my household with the blood of Jesus Christ.
10. My prayers today will not go in vain; my prayers will produce the desired results in the name of Jesus Christ.
11. According to the Word of God, I am a lawful owner of all things. Today, I claim all that belongs to me, in the name of Jesus Christ.
12. I am a lawful owner of all things. Today, I claim the riches and wealth of this world, in the name of Jesus Christ.
13. I am a lawful owner of all things. I refuse to die in poverty, in the name of Jesus Christ.
14. I am a lawful owner of all things. Father, let the blessings of heaven be released to me now, in the name of Jesus Christ.
15. I am a lawful owner of all things. Father Lord, let my prosperity manifest now, in the name of Jesus Christ.
16. I am a lawful owner of all things. Father Lord, let my breakthroughs manifest now, in the name of Jesus Christ.

17. I am a lawful owner of all things. Why do I have to suffer? I reject sufferings in every area of my life, in the name of Jesus Christ.
18. I am a lawful owner of all things. I refuse to labor in vain, in the name of Jesus Christ.
19. I am a lawful owner of all things. I refuse to fish in the Dead Sea, in the name of Jesus Christ.
20. I am a lawful owner of all things. I refuse to fish in the wrong water, in the name of Jesus Christ.
21. I am a lawful owner of all things. I refuse to labor for another to eat, in the name of Jesus Christ.
22. I am a lawful owner of all things. No matter the situation, I will not beg for bread, in the name of Jesus Christ.
23. I am a lawful owner of all things. No matter the situation I will not lack any good things, in the name of Jesus Christ.
24. I am a lawful owner of all things. Today I decree that money will not run away from me, in the name of Jesus Christ.
25. I am a lawful owner of all things. Today I decree that my promotion will not be given to another person, in the name of Jesus Christ.
26. I am a lawful owner of all things. Today I decree that prosperity will not run away from me, in the name of Jesus Christ.
27. I am a lawful owner of all things. Father Lord, let divine supplies be always available unto me, in the name of Jesus Christ.
28. I am a lawful owner of all things. Today I receive divine protection over me and my household, in the name of Jesus Christ.

29. I am a lawful owner of all things. Let there be open heavens and super-abundance released into my life, in the name of Jesus Christ.
30. I am a lawful owner of all things. Let there be open heavens, and super-abundance released into my finances, in the name of Jesus Christ.
31. I am a lawful owner of all things. Let there be open heavens and super-abundance released into my family, in the name of Jesus Christ.
32. I am a lawful owner of all things. Today I receive divine assistance to achieve my goals, in the name of Jesus Christ.
33. I am a lawful owner of all things. Today I receive divine assistance to fulfill my dreams, in the name of Jesus Christ.
34. I am a lawful owner of all things. Today I receive divine assistance to pay my bills, in the name of Jesus Christ.
35. I am a lawful owner of all things. Today I receive divine assistance to move to the top of the ladder, in the name of Jesus Christ.
36. I am a lawful owner of all things. Today I receive divine assistance to move forward in every area of my life, in the name of Jesus Christ.
37. I am a lawful owner of all things. I hereby command poverty to get out of my life, in the name of Jesus Christ.
38. I am a lawful owner of all things. I hereby command lack to depart from me; we have nothing in common, in the name of Jesus Christ.
39. I am a lawful owner of all things. I hereby command failure to get out of my life, in the name of Jesus Christ.

40. I am a lawful owner of all things. I command every limitation on progress to be removed now by the fire of God, in the name of Jesus Christ.

41. I am a lawful owner of all things. I command every limitation on promotion to be removed now by the fire of God, in the name of Jesus Christ.

42. I am a lawful owner of all things. Let your good treasures be opened unto me today O Lord, in the name of Jesus Christ.

43. I am a lawful owner of all things. Let the wealth of this world be given unto me O Lord, in the name of Jesus Christ.

44. I am a lawful owner of all things. Let the wealth of Gentiles be given unto me O Lord, in the name of Jesus Christ.

45. I am a lawful owner of all things. I command the rich and wealthy of this world to locate me now and give me financial support, in the name of Jesus Christ.

46. I am a lawful owner of all things. I command the great and mighty people of the world to locate me now and give me financial support, in the name of Jesus Christ.

47. I am a lawful owner of all things. I command men and women all around me to come together to give me financial support, in the name of Jesus Christ.

48. I am a lawful owner of all things. I command people that I know and people that I don't know to come and give me financial support, in the name of Jesus Christ.

49. I am a lawful owner of all things. Today I tap into milk and honey flowing in this land, in the name of Jesus Christ.

50. I am a lawful owner of all things. I command the treasures of darkness to be released unto me now, in the name of Jesus Christ.
51. I am a lawful owner of all things. I command the hidden riches of secret places to be released unto me now, in the name of Jesus Christ.
52. I am a lawful owner of all things. I command all good things stolen from me to be released back unto me now, in the name of Jesus Christ.
53. I am a lawful owner of all things. I command my stolen blessings to be released unto me now, in the name of Jesus Christ.
54. I am a lawful owner of all things. I command my hindered breakthroughs to be released now, in the name of Jesus Christ.
55. I am a lawful owner of all things. I command every door of brass blocking my breakthroughs to be destroyed now, in the name of Jesus Christ.
56. I am a lawful owner of all things. I command every door of brass blocking my miracles to be destroyed now, in the name of Jesus Christ.
57. I am a lawful owner of all things. I command every door of brass blocking my promotion to be destroyed now, in the name of Jesus Christ.
58. I am a lawful owner of all things. I command every door of brass blocking my advancement to be destroyed now, in the name of Jesus Christ.
59. I am a lawful owner of all things. I command every door of brass blocking my expansion to be destroyed now, in the name of Jesus Christ.

60. I am a lawful owner of all things. I command every door of brass blocking my supernatural increase to be destroyed now, in the name of Jesus Christ.

I cover my prayers in the blood of Jesus Christ. According to the Word of God, I have asked, I shall receive. I have knocked the door, it shall be opened unto me. I have sought, I shall find, in the name of Jesus Christ. It is written, "… Decree a thing, and it shall be established". As I have spoken in prayer, it shall be so. My prayers shall produce desire results. My prayers shall produce desired miracles. My prayers shall produce desired testimonies, in the name of Jesus Christ. Territorial spirit and power cannot hinder this prayer. Sins and flesh cannot hinder this prayer. It is done. It is sealed by the blood of Jesus Christ. It is delivered to me, in Jesus might name. Amen!

DAY EIGHT

PRAYER FOR GOD TO MAKE A WAY WHEN ALL DOORS ARE SHUT AGAINST YOU

Passages To Read Before You Pray:
Deuteronomy 2:14-15, Hebrews 12:15, Colossians 2:14,
Psalms 103, 105, 106

In the book of Job 22:28, the Scripture says when I decree a thing, it shall be established for me. I stand on this Scripture and decree. I have come today to fellowship with my heavenly Father, and make my requests and needs known unto Him. I cannot be hindered nor delayed because I know who I am in the Lord. I am a child of the Kingdom, born of the Spirit, redeemed by the blood of Jesus Christ. I walk in authority, living life without any apology because the power and authority has been given to me according to the Word of God in the book of Luke 9:1.

As I have come to pray today and to fellowship with my heavenly Father, I cover myself in the blood of Jesus Christ, and I put on the whole armor of God. I hereby come against every Prince of Persia that wants to hinder my prayer, I arrest you by the power in the blood of Jesus Christ, and I bind you and cast you down into the pit of hell.

I come against principalities and powers that wrestle with me and my prayers, I arrest you today by the power in the name of Jesus Christ, and I bind you and cast down into the pit of hell. I come against the rulers of the darkness of this world, against spiritual wickedness in high places, I arrest you all by the power in the name of Jesus Christ, and I bind you and cast you down into the pit of hell. I come against weakness and weariness, I

arrest you today by the power in the name of Jesus Christ, and I bind you and cast you out of my life. I come against wondering spirit and distractions, I arrest you today by the power in the name of Jesus Christ, and I bind you and cast you out of my life.

Today I receive the anointing to pray and get results, my prayers cannot be hindered nor delayed because Jesus is my Lord, I will pray today and get the desired results, I decree open heavens upon my prayers. I baptize myself in the fire of the Holy Ghost; therefore I have become too hot for the enemy to handle. My prayers today will attract divine intervention to every situation in my life; signs and wonders will follow my prayers today, testimonies will follow my prayers today and the name of God alone will be glorified, in Jesus name. Amen!

PRAYER POINTS

1. O God my Father, thank you for being my God, my Father and my friend.
2. O God my Father, thank you for the privilege to know you and the power of the resurrection of Jesus Christ.
3. O God my Father, thank you for always being there for me and with me.
4. O God my Father, thank you for the great and mighty things that you are doing in my life.
5. O God my Father, thank you for your provision and protection over me and my household.
6. O God my Father, thank you for always answering my prayers.

7. I confess my sins before you today and I ask you to forgive me on the basis of your mercy, in the name of Jesus Christ.

8. Wash me clean today O Lord by the blood of Jesus Christ.

9. I cover myself and my household with the blood of Jesus Christ.

10. My prayers today will not go in vain; my prayers will produce the desired results in the name of Jesus Christ.

11. Anything in my life making me a target of satanic attacks, be destroyed by the fire of God.

12. Anything in my life making me a target of spiritual bullies is destroyed by the fire of God.

13. Every handwriting contrary to the will and the purpose of God for me is erased by the blood of Jesus Christ.

14. Evil handwriting upon my life attracting hatred and failure, be erased by the blood of Jesus.

15. Every mark of rejection upon my life causing me to be rejected wherever I go, be removed now by the blood of Jesus Christ.

16. O God my Father, make a way for me out of this wilderness of trouble that I find myself.

17. O God my Father, for how long will I wander in this wilderness of disappointment, arise and make a way for me out of this wilderness.

18. Any power anywhere trying to turn the journey of ten days to ten years for me, you will not prosper, and you will not escape the judgment of God.

19. O God my Father, for how long will I suffer before I get to my promise land, arise O Lord and expedite my progress.

20. O God my Father, let the spirit and the anointing of Caleb rest upon me, the boldness to possess my possessions.
21. I refuse to be afraid of giants; I receive power to possess my possessions.
22. O God my Father, send your fire to the root of my problems and let it be destroyed from the root.
23. O God my Father, let the root of bitterness in my life be destroyed by your fire.
24. O God my Father, send your fire to the root of frustration in my life, and let it be destroyed by your fire.
25. I refuse to be frustrated.
26. In your presence O Lord, my case will not be impossible.

I cover my prayers in the blood of Jesus Christ. According to the Word of God, I have asked; I shall receive. I have knocked the door; it shall be opened unto me. I have sought; I shall find, in the name of Jesus Christ. It is written, "… Decree a thing, and it shall be established". As I have spoken in prayer, it shall be so. My prayers shall produce desired results. My prayers shall produce desired miracles. My prayers shall produce desired testimonies, in the name of Jesus Christ. Territorial spirit and power cannot hinder this prayer. Sins and flesh cannot hinder this prayer. It is done. It is sealed by the blood of Jesus Christ. It is delivered to me, in Jesus mighty name. Amen!

DAY NINE

PRAYER FOR DIVINE CONNECTIONS

Passages To Read Before You Pray:
Proverbs 18:16, Ruth 2:11-12, 1 Samuel 18:1,
Psalms 78, 115, 42, 19

In the book of Job 22:28, the Scripture says when I decree a thing, it shall be established for me. I stand on this Scripture and decree. I have come into the presence of God today to plead my case. I enter through the gate of praise, into the sanctuary of heaven. I cover myself in the precious blood of Jesus Christ. I baptize myself in the fire of the Holy Ghost. I charge this atmosphere with the fire of God, and I take this neighborhood for the Lord. I arrest every principality and power, territorial spirit, and every throne and kingdom that is not of God. I cast you down and I command you never to lift yourself up against me, because I have the life of God in me.

In the name of Jesus Christ, I confess my sins today, and I ask you O Lord to forgive me on the basis of your mercy. With all my heart, I forgive those who have sinned against me; from the past through this moment. I release them from any form of guilt and shame, in the name of Jesus Christ. I hereby plead the blood of Jesus over any sins committed by my parents and ancestors. I cancel through the Blood of Jesus Christ, any satanic covenants, exchanges, vows or transactions, made over my life, body, soul, spirit, and circumstances, in the name of Jesus Christ. I cancel every legal right that the devil may have against me, by the blood of Jesus Christ. The accuser of the brethren will have nothing against me, as I come to the presence of God in prayer.

The devil cannot hinder or delay my prayer, because I know who I am. I am a child of the Kingdom. I am a king and priest of the Lord, redeemed from the hand of the devil by the blood of Jesus Christ. I walk in power. I walk in miracle. Proverbs 18:21 says, death and life are in the power of my tongue; I command the power in my tongue to manifest now. I command my tongue to become fire, to consume all the powers of darkness in the air, the land, the sea, and beneath the earth. I hereby raise Holy Ghost standard against the prince of the power of the air and all the hosts of darkness in the air. I raise Holy Ghost standard against the queen of the coasts and all the hosts of darkness on the land. I raise Holy Ghost standard against the marine kingdom and all the hosts of darkness in the sea. I raise Holy Ghost standard against the kingdom of hell and all the hosts of darkness beneath the earth. I shoot down all the networks of demons gathering to resist my prayers. I rebuke and bind all the controlling forces of darkness standing against my prayers.

I declare that all satanic thrones, altars, dominions, principalities, powers, rulers of darkness, queens of the coast, queens of heavens, household wickedness, spiritual hosts of wickedness and all satanic works, have no power or authority over my life. I declare that satanic harassment and intimidation have no effect on me.

Today, I receive divine strength to pray; I will not pray in vain. I will not pray amiss. My prayers will bring the desired results. I command the fountain of prayer to open now, and to flow into my life, I command the warring angels of God to descend and fight on my behalf. Every minute and every hour that I spend in prayer, will bring solution. Every prayer point will attract divine attention and divine intervention. I decree open heavens over my

prayers, and today, God of heaven and earth will attend to my case. My prayers today will shake the heavens and move the earth. Testimonies, miracles, healings, breakthroughs, and signs and wonders, will follow my prayers. At the end of this prayer session, my life will never be the same again.

PRAYER POINTS

1. O God my Father, thank you for being my God, my Father and my friend.
2. O God my Father, thank you for the privilege to know you and the power of the resurrection of Jesus Christ.
3. O God my Father, thank you for always being there for me and with me.
4. O God my Father, thank you for the great and mighty things that you are doing in my life.
5. O God my Father, thank you for your provision and protection over me and my household.
6. O God my Father, thank you for always answering my prayers.
7. I confess my sins before you today and I ask you to forgive me on the basis of your mercy, in the name of Jesus Christ.
8. Wash me clean today O Lord by the blood of Jesus Christ.
9. I cover myself and my household with the blood of Jesus Christ.
10. My prayers today will not go in vain; my prayers will produce the desired results in the name of Jesus Christ.
11. O God my Father, let doors of unusual connection be opened unto me now, in the name of Jesus Christ.

12. O God my Father, by your mighty hands, connect me to those that will lift up my destiny, in the name of Jesus Christ.

13. O God my Father, by your mighty hands, connect me to those that will lift up my family, in the name of Jesus Christ.

14. O God my Father, by your mighty hands, connect me to those that will lift up my hands, in the name of Jesus Christ.

15. O God my Father, by your mighty hands, connect me to those that will lift up my head, in the name of Jesus Christ.

16. O God my Father, by your mighty hands, connect me to those that will lift me up to a higher ground, in the name of Jesus Christ.

17. O God my Father, by your mighty hands, connect me to those that you have prepared to help me in life, in the name of Jesus Christ.

18. O God my Father, by your mighty hands, connect me to those that will show me how to make it in life, in the name of Jesus Christ.

19. O God my Father, by your mighty hands, connect me to those that will lead me to my promise land, in the name of Jesus Christ.

20. O God my Father, by your mighty hands, connect me to those that will show me the secret of how to make wealth, in the name of Jesus Christ.

21. O God my Father, by your mighty hands, connect me to those that will lead me to the top, in the name of Jesus Christ.

22. O God my Father, rightly connect me to men and women who will help me in life, in the name of Jesus

Christ.

23. O God my Father, rightly connect me to men and women who will help me that my business may flourish, in the name of Jesus Christ.

24. O God my Father, rightly connect me to men and women who will help me that my ministry may prosper, in the name of Jesus Christ.

25. O God my Father, rightly connect me to men and women who will help me to become what I am created to be, in the name of Jesus Christ.

26. O God my Father, rightly connect me to men and women who will put me in the right path to success, in the name of Jesus Christ.

27. O God my Father, rightly connect me to men and women in high places, in the name of Jesus Christ.

28. Proverbs 18:16 says, the gift of a man makes room for him; I command the gift of God in me to manifest now for the world to see, in the name of Jesus Christ.

29. Proverbs 18:16 says, the gift of a man makes room for him; I command the gift of God in me to make room for me wherever I go, in the name of Jesus Christ.

30. Proverbs 18:16 says, the gift of a man makes room for him; I command the gift of God in me to make room for me wherever I find myself, in the name of Jesus Christ.

31. Proverbs 18:16 says, the gift of a man makes room for him; I command the gift of God in me to make a way for me, where there is no way, in the name of Jesus Christ.

32. Proverbs 18:16 says, the gift of a man makes room for him; I command the gift of God in me to attract kings and queens to me, in the name of Jesus Christ.

33. Proverbs 18:16 says, the gift of a man makes room for him; I command the gift of God in me to attract princes

and princesses to me, in the name of Jesus Christ.

34. Proverbs 18:16 says, the gift of a man makes room for him; I command the gift of God in me to attract presidents and governors to me, in the name of Jesus Christ.

35. Proverbs 18:16 says, the gift of a man brings him before great men; I command the gift of God in me to divinely connect me to great men all over the world, in the name of Jesus Christ.

36. Proverbs 18:16 says, the gift of a man brings him before great men; I command the gift of God in me to divinely connect me to great women all over the world, in the name of Jesus Christ.

37. Proverbs 18:16 says, the gift of a man brings him before great men; I command the gift of God in me to divinely connect me to men and women in high places, in the name of Jesus Christ.

38. Proverbs 18:16 says, the gift of a man brings him before great men; I command the gift of God in me to divinely connect me to multi-millionaires all over the world, in the name of Jesus Christ.

39. Proverbs 18:16 says, the gift of a man brings him before great men; I command the gift of God in me to divinely connect me to multi-billionaires all over the world, in the name of Jesus Christ.

40. Proverbs 18:16 says, the gift of a man brings him before great men; I command the gift of God in me to divinely connect me to CEOs of large corporations all over the world, in the name of Jesus Christ.

41. Proverbs 18:16 says, the gift of a man brings him before great men; I command the gift of God in me to divinely connect me to my helpers all over the world, in the name

of Jesus Christ.

42. Proverbs 18:16 says, the gift of a man brings him before great men; I command the gift of God in me to divinely connect me to those that God had prepared to help me, in the name of Jesus Christ.

43. O God my Father, arise and rightly connect me to kings and queens that will bless me, in the name of Jesus Christ.

44. O God my Father, arise and position me to be in the right place, at the right time, to meet my divine helpers, in the name of Jesus Christ.

45. I stand on the Word of God. I receive divine connection that will change my story for good forever, in the name of Jesus Christ.

46. I stand on the Word of God. I receive divine connection that will change my status for good forever, in the name of Jesus Christ.

47. I stand on the Word of God. I receive divine connection that will change my destiny for the better, in the name of Jesus Christ.

48. I stand on the Word of God. I receive divine connection that will change my friends for the better, in the name of Jesus Christ.

49. I stand on the Word of God. I receive divine connection that will change my company for the better, in the name of Jesus Christ.

50. I stand on the Word of God. I receive divine connection that will change my neighborhood for the better, in the name of Jesus Christ.

51. I stand on the Word of God. I receive divine connection that will change my vocabulary for the better, in the name of Jesus Christ.

52. O God my Father, connect me to the right people that will connect me to the right business, in the name of Jesus Christ.

53. O God my Father, connect me to my financial breakthrough this year, in the name of Jesus Christ.

54. O God my Father, connect me to my spiritual breakthrough this year, in the name of Jesus Christ.

55. O God my Father, let international doors of opportunity be open unto me now, in the name of Jesus Christ.

56. I stand on the Word of God. I receive divine connection to my benefactors now, in the name of Jesus Christ.

57. I stand on the Word of God. I receive divine connection to men and women that will support my vision, in the name of Jesus Christ.

58. I stand on the Word of God. I receive divine connection to men and women that will support my dreams, in the name of Jesus Christ.

59. I stand on the Word of God. I receive divine connection to men and women that will support my good efforts, in the name of Jesus Christ.

60. I stand on the Word of God. I reject wrong connections and deceptions of the devil, in the name of Jesus Christ.

61. O God my Father, connect me to my spiritual counselor, in the name of Jesus Christ.

62. O God my Father, connect me to my spiritual counselor that you have chosen to be a spiritual covering to me, in the name of Jesus Christ.

63. O God my Father, connect me to men and women that will help my ministry, in the name of Jesus Christ.

64. O God my Father, connect me to men and women that will help my career, in the name of Jesus Christ.

I cover my prayers in the blood of Jesus Christ. According to the Word of God, I have asked; I shall receive. I have knocked the door; it shall be opened unto me. I have sought; I shall find, in the name of Jesus Christ. It is written, "… Decree a thing, and it shall be established". As I have spoken in prayer, it shall be so. My prayers shall produce desired results. My prayers shall produce desired miracles. My prayers shall produce desired testimonies, in the name of Jesus Christ. Territorial spirit and power cannot hinder this prayer. Sins and flesh cannot hinder this prayer. It is done. It is sealed by the blood of Jesus Christ. It is delivered to me, in Jesus mighty name. Amen!

DAY TEN

PRAYER TO OVERCOME OBSTACLES
IN YOUR WAY

Passages To Read Before You Pray:
Exodus 14:1-14, Isaiah 45:2-3, Psalms 46, 10, 118

In the book of Job 22:28, the Scripture says when I decree a thing, it shall be established for me. I stand on this Scripture and decree. I have come today to fellowship with my heavenly Father, and make my requests and needs known unto Him. I cannot be hindered nor delayed because I know who I am in the Lord. I am a child of the Kingdom, born of the Spirit, redeemed by the blood of Jesus Christ. I walk in authority, living life without any apology because the power and authority has been given to me according to the Word of God in the book of Luke 9:1.

As I have come to pray today and to fellowship with my heavenly Father, I cover myself in the blood of Jesus Christ, and I put on the whole armor of God. I hereby come against every Prince of Persia that wants to hinder my prayer, I arrest you by the power in the blood of Jesus Christ, and I bind you and cast you down into the pit of hell.

I come against principalities and powers that wrestle with me and my prayers, I arrest you today by the power in the name of Jesus Christ, and I bind you and cast down into the pit of hell. I come against the rulers of the darkness of this world, against spiritual wickedness in high places, I arrest you all by the power in the name of Jesus Christ, and I bind you and cast you down into the pit of hell. I come against weakness and weariness, I arrest you today by the power in the name of Jesus Christ, and I

bind you and cast you out of my life. I come against wondering spirit and distractions, I arrest you today by the power in the name of Jesus Christ, and I bind you and cast you out of my life.

Today I receive the anointing to pray and get results, my prayers cannot be hindered nor delayed because Jesus is my Lord, I will pray today and get the desired results, I decree open heavens upon my prayers. I baptize myself in the fire of the Holy Ghost; therefore I have become too hot for the enemy to handle. My prayers today will attract divine intervention to every situation in my life; signs and wonders will follow my prayers today, testimonies will follow my prayers today and the name of God alone will be glorified, in Jesus name. Amen!

PRAYER POINTS

1. O God my Father, thank you for being my God, my Father and my friend.
2. O God my Father, thank you for the privilege to know you and the power of the resurrection of Jesus Christ.
3. O God my Father, thank you for always being there for me and with me.
4. O God my Father, thank you for the great and mighty things that you are doing in my life.
5. O God my Father, thank you for your provision and protection over me and my household.
6. O God my Father, thank you for always answering my prayers.
7. I confess my sins before you today and I ask you to forgive me on the basis of your mercy, in the name of Jesus Christ.

8. Wash me clean today O Lord by the blood of Jesus Christ.

9. I cover myself and my household with the blood of Jesus Christ.

10. My prayers today will not go in vain; my prayers will produce the desired results in the name of Jesus Christ.

11. By the power in the name of Jesus Christ, I command Red Sea on my way to give way right now, I am crossing over.

12. By the power in the name of Jesus Christ, I command every Red Sea that wants to keep me in the Egyptian bondage, to dry up.

13. By the power in the name of Jesus Christ, I command every Red Sea that wants me to die in Egypt to give way now.

14. By the power in the name of Jesus Christ, I command the Red Sea on my way to swallow my stubborn pursuers.

15. O God my Father, send the east wind today and divide the Red Sea on my way so that I may cross over to my promise land.

16. O ye Red Sea on the way to my promise land, I command you to cooperate with the divine agenda for my life.

17. O ye Red Sea on the way to my promise land, you cannot stop me I am a child of the King, give way now.

18. O ye Red Sea on the way to my promise land, you cannot hinder me I am a child of the King, give way now.

19. O ye Red Sea on the way to my promise land, you cannot delay me I am a child of the King, give way now.

20. Any power anywhere expecting me to die in the wilderness of hopelessness, you will not escape the judgment of God. (Ex. 14:3)

21. Any power anywhere expecting me to die in the wilderness of problem, you will not escape the judgment of God.

22. Any power anywhere expecting me to die in the wilderness of poverty, you will not escape the judgment of God.

23. Any power anywhere expecting me to die in the wilderness of suffering, you will not escape the judgment of God.

24. Any power anywhere expecting me to die in the wilderness of confusion, you will not escape the judgment of God.

25. Any power anywhere expecting me to die in the wilderness of ignorance, you will not escape the judgment of God.

26. Any power anywhere expecting me to die in the wilderness of sadness and bitterness, you will not escape the judgment of God.

27. Any power anywhere expecting me to die in the wilderness of lack, you will not escape the judgment of God.

28. Any power anywhere pursuing me in order to enslave me, fall today, you and your army in the order of Pharaoh. (Ex. 14:5-9)

29. Any power anywhere pursuing me in order to destroy the works of my hand, fall today, you and your army in the order of Pharaoh.

30. Household wickedness pursuing me in order to hinder the plan of God for my life, you will not escape the judgment of God.

31. Anybody anywhere pursuing me in order to stop what God is doing in my life, be disappointed today because you cannot stop God.

32. Anybody anywhere pursuing me in order to fulfill his desire upon my life, I command you to fail, my case is different.

33. O God my Father, when I am confused and don't know what to do, let there be divine intervention in every area of my life.

34. O God my Father, when all hope is lost and my faith is weak, arise and carry me in your arm.

35. O God my Father, when I am weak and don't have the strength to pray, let your grace be sufficient for me.

36. O God my Father, when all roads are closed and darkness covers my way, let your light shine and make a way where there seems to be no way.

37. O God my Father, deliver me today from the hands of Pharaoh that wants to keep me in bondage.

38. No matter the situation around me, I will not die in Egypt.

39. Arise O Lord and sign my release form today, I am getting out of this bondage.

40. Arise O Lord and sign my release form today, I am getting out of this stubborn situation.

41. Arise O Lord and sign my release form today, I am getting out of this hopeless situation.

42. Arise O Lord and sign my release form today, I am getting out of this problem.

43. Arise O Lord and sign my release form today, I am getting out of this financial mess.

44. Arise O Lord and sign my release form today, I am getting out of this shameful situation.

45. Arise O Lord and sign my release form today, I am getting out of this wilderness.

46. As I lift up my voice in prayer today, let my stubborn situation tremble and bow at the name of Jesus Christ. (James 2:19)(Philippians 2:9-11)

47. As I lift up my voice in prayer today, let my stubborn enemy tremble and bow at the name of Jesus Christ.

48. As I lift up my voice in prayer today, let my household wickedness tremble and bow at the name of Jesus Christ.

49. As I lift up my voice in prayer today, let the power assigned to hinder my prayers tremble and bow at the name of Jesus Christ.

50. As I lift up my voice in prayer today, let the power assigned to stop my breakthrough tremble and bow at the name of Jesus Christ.

51. As I lift up my voice in prayer today, let the power assigned to delay my promotion tremble and bow at the name of Jesus Christ.

52. As I lift up my voice in prayer today, let the power assigned to attack my joy tremble and bow at the name of Jesus Christ.

53. As I lift up my voice in prayer today, let the power assigned to my marriage tremble and bow at the name of Jesus Christ.

54. As I lift up my voice in prayer today, let the power assigned to attack my finances tremble and bow at the name of Jesus Christ.

55. As I lift up my voice in prayer today, let the power of sickness in my life tremble and bow at the name of Jesus Christ.

56. As I lift up my voice in prayer today, let the power of poverty in my life tremble and bow at the name of Jesus Christ.

57. Today O Lord, let every mountain of problem in my life disappear.

58. Today O Lord, let every ocean of problem in my life disappear.

59. Today O Lord, let every wilderness of problem in my life disappear.

60. Today O Lord, let every cloud of problem over my life clear away.

I cover my prayers in the blood of Jesus Christ. According to the Word of God, I have asked; I shall receive. I have knocked the door; it shall be opened unto me. I have sought; I shall find, in the name of Jesus Christ. It is written, "... Decree a thing, and it shall be established". As I have spoken in prayer, it shall be so. My prayers shall produce desired results. My prayers shall produce desired miracles. My prayers shall produce desired testimonies, in the name of Jesus Christ. Territorial spirit and power cannot hinder this prayer. Sins and flesh cannot hinder this prayer. It is done. It is sealed by the blood of Jesus Christ. It is delivered to me, in Jesus mighty name. Amen!

DAY ELEVEN

PRAYER TO BREAK CYCLE
OF FAILURE

Passages To Read Before You Pray:
Galatians 3:13, Joshua 1:1-18, Psalms 46, 86, 29, 59. 69

In the book of Job 22:28, the Scripture says when I decree a thing, it shall be established for me. I stand on this Scripture and decree. I claim my right as a child of the Kingdom, I cover myself in the blood of Jesus Christ, I cover my household and everything concerning me in the blood of Jesus Christ. I hereby charge this atmosphere by the blood of Jesus Christ and by the fire of the Holy Ghost. I command fresh fire of God to rest upon me now as in the day of Pentecost, let fresh anointing and new oil be released upon me now as I pray. I receive power and authority over the power and the kingdom of darkness, to root out and to pull down, to destroy and to throw down, to build and to plant; whatever I decree in this prayer shall be established; whatever I bind today shall be bound in heaven and whatever I loose today shall be loosed in heaven as it is written in the word of God. Let fresh fire of God be released on my prayer altar and my prayer life now, prince of Persia cannot hinder my prayer, territorial spirit of my neighborhood cannot hinder my prayer, household wickedness cannot hinder my prayer.

I can see my prayer attracting divine intervention. This is the day that the Lord has made, I will rejoice and be glad in it. This is the day that the Lord has chosen to set me free from any form of bondage and break any form of curses upon my life; this is the day that I will receive a total and complete deliverance in every area of my life, today shall mark the beginning of a new thing in my life.

I am a child of God, born of the Spirit, redeemed by the blood of the Lamb. It is written concerning me that power and authority is given unto me over all devils and to cure diseases, I hereby take authority over any form of curses upon my life, be it ancestral, be it generational, be it demon-inflicted or self-inflicted; I command all curses upon my life to break now by the authority in the name of Jesus Christ. The Bible says, where the word of a king is, there is power; today I speak as a king with the authority and power of the King of kings, and I command every other power to bow in the name of Jesus Christ. I render any power behind any curse upon my life useless and ineffective; I overcome any form of distraction, spiritual laziness and slumber, before the end of this prayer session my testimonies shall manifest without delay by the power in the name of Jesus Christ. Amen!

PRAYER POINTS

1. God my Father, thank you for being my God, my Father and my friend.
2. God my Father, thank you for the privilege to know you and the power of the resurrection of Jesus Christ.
3. God my Father, thank you for always being there for me and with me.
4. God my Father, thank you for the great and mighty things that you are doing in my life.
5. God my Father, thank you for your provision and protection over me and my household.

6. God my Father, thank you for always answering my prayers.
7. I confess my sins before you today and I ask you to forgive me on the basis of your mercy, in the name of Jesus Christ.
8. Wash me clean today O Lord by the blood of Jesus Christ.
9. I cover myself and my household with the blood of Jesus Christ.
10. My prayers today will not go in vain; my prayers will produce the desired results in the name of Jesus Christ.
11. I take authority and break every curse of failure upon my life in the name of Jesus Christ.
12. By the power in the of blood of Jesus Christ I break every curse of failure in my bloodline from my life to my past generations all the way to Adam the first man, in the name of Jesus Christ.
13. By the power in the blood of Jesus Christ I break every curse of failure over my children and their children and children's children, in the name of Jesus Christ.
14. I take authority and break the curse of failure at the edge of miracle, in the name of Jesus Christ.
15. I take authority and break every curse of failure at the point of breakthrough, in the name of Jesus Christ.
16. I take authority and break every curse of failure holding my life down, in the name of Jesus Christ.
17. I take authority and break every curse of failure causing my life to be stagnated, in the name of Jesus Christ.
18. I take authority and break every curse of failure causing my life to go backward, in the name of Jesus Christ.
19. I take authority and break every curse of failure causing me to live a miserable life, in the name of Jesus Christ.

20. I take authority and break every curse of failure causing me to lose every opportunity that comes my way, in the name of Jesus Christ.
21. I take authority and break every curse of failure causing me to lose divine helpers that God has sent to help me, in the name of Jesus Christ.
22. I take authority and break every curse of failure keeping me at the bottom of the ladder, in the name of Jesus Christ.
23. I take authority and break every cycle of failure in any area of my life, in the name of Jesus Christ.
24. I take authority and break every cycle of failure in marriage, in the name of Jesus Christ.
25. I take authority and break every cycle of failure manifesting in the life of my spouse in the name of Jesus Christ.
26. I take authority and break every cycle of failure manifesting in the life of my children, in the name of Jesus Christ.
27. I take authority and break every cycle of failure manifesting in my business, in the name of Jesus Christ.
28. I take authority and break every cycle of failure manifesting in my finances, in the name of Jesus Christ.
29. I take authority and break every cycle of failure concerning all my relationships, in the name of Jesus Christ.
30. I take authority and break every cycle of failure that will not allow me to get marry, in the name of Jesus Christ.
31. I take authority and break every cycle of failure that will not allow me to have a successful and stable relationship, in the name of Jesus Christ.

32. I take authority and break every cycle of failure that will not allow me to have a good and stable employment, in the name of Jesus Christ.

33. Every curse of last minute failure, enough is enough, I command you to break now by the power in the name of Jesus Christ.

34. Every curse of last minute failure in the life of my spouse, enough is enough, I command you to break now by the power in the name of Jesus Christ.

35. Every curse of last minute failure in the life of my children, enough is enough, I command you to break now by the power in the name of Jesus Christ.

36. Every curse of last minute failure in my finances, enough is enough, I command you to break now by the power in the name of Jesus Christ.

37. Every curse of last minute failure working against my breakthrough, enough is enough, I command you to break now by the power in the name of Jesus Christ.

38. Every curse of last minute failure working against my miracles, enough is enough, I command you to break now by the power in the name of Jesus Christ.

I cover my prayers in the blood of Jesus Christ. According to the Word of God, I have asked; I shall receive. I have knocked the door; it shall be opened unto me. I have sought; I shall find, in the name of Jesus Christ. It is written, "… Decree a thing, and it shall be established". As I have spoken in prayer, it shall be so. My prayers shall produce desired results. My prayers shall produce desired miracles. My prayers shall produce desired testimonies, in the name of Jesus Christ. Territorial spirit and power cannot hinder this prayer. Sins and flesh cannot hinder this prayer. It is done. It is sealed by the blood of Jesus Christ. It is delivered to me, in Jesus mighty name. Amen!

DAY TWELVE

LET THERE BE DIVINE GREEN LIGHT

Passages To Read Before You Pray:

Exodus 13:18-22, Genesis 1:1-3, Isaiah 43:19, Isaiah 30:21, Isaiah 45:2-3, Psalms 42, 83, 99

In the book of Job 22:28, the Scripture says when I decree a thing, it shall be established for me. I stand on this Scripture and decree. I have come into the presence of God today to plead my case. I enter through the gate of praise into the sanctuary of heaven. I cover myself in the precious blood of Jesus Christ. I baptize myself in the fire of the Holy Ghost. I charge this atmosphere with the fire of God, and I take this neighborhood for the Lord. I arrest every principality and power, territorial spirit, and every throne and kingdom that is not of God. I cast you down and I command you never to lift yourself up against me, because I have the life of God in me.

In the name of Jesus Christ, I confess my sins today, and I ask you O Lord to forgive me on the basis of your mercy. With all my heart, I forgive those who have sinned against me from the past through this moment. I release them from any form of guilt and shame, in the name of Jesus Christ. I hereby plead the blood of Jesus over any sins committed by my parents and ancestors. I cancel through the Blood of Jesus Christ, any satanic covenants, exchanges, vows or transactions made over my life, body, soul, spirit, and circumstances, in the name of Jesus Christ. I cancel every legal right that the devil may have against me, by the blood of Jesus Christ. The accuser of the brethren will have nothing against me as I come to the presence of God in prayer.

The devil cannot hinder or delay my prayer, because I know who I am. I am a child of the Kingdom; I am a king and priest of the Lord, redeemed from the hand of the devil by the blood of Jesus Christ. I declare that all satanic thrones, altars, dominions, principalities, powers, rulers of darkness, queen of the coast, queen of heavens, household wickedness, spiritual hosts of wickedness and all satanic works, have no power or authority over my life. I declare that satanic harassment and intimidation have no effect on me.

Today I receive divine strength to pray; I will not pray in vain. I will not pray amiss. My prayers will bring the desired results. I command the fountain of prayer to open now, and flow into my life, I command the warring angels of God to descend and fight on my behalf. Every minute and every hour that I spend in prayer will bring solution. Every prayer point will attract divine attention and divine intervention. I decree open heavens over my prayers, and today, God of heaven and earth will attend to my case. My prayers today will shake the heavens and move the earth; testimonies, miracles, healing, breakthrough, signs and wonders will follow my prayers. At the end of this prayer session, my life will never be the same again.

PRAYER POINTS

1. O God my Father, thank you for being my God, my Father and my friend.
2. O God my Father, thank you for the privilege to know you and the power of the resurrection of Jesus Christ.
3. O God my Father, thank you for always being there for me and with me.

4. O God my Father, thank you for the great and mighty things that you are doing in my life.
5. O God my Father, thank you for your provision and protection over me and my household.
6. O God my Father, thank you for always answering my prayers.
7. I confess my sins before you today and I ask you to forgive me on the basis of your mercy, in the name of Jesus Christ.
8. Wash me clean today O Lord by the blood of Jesus Christ.
9. I cover myself and my household with the blood of Jesus Christ.
10. My prayers today will not go in vain; my prayers will produce the desired results in the name of Jesus Christ.
11. O God my Father, let there be divine green light in every area of my life, in the name of Jesus Christ.
12. O God my Father, let there be divine green light concerning my goals and dreams, in the name of Jesus Christ.
13. O God my Father, let there be divine green light in every area of my business, in the name of Jesus Christ.
14. O God my Father, let there be divine green light concerning that which I set my mind on doing, in the name of Jesus Christ.
15. O God my Father, let there be divine green light concerning all my life proposals, in the name of Jesus Christ.
16. O God my Father, let there be divine green light concerning my marriage, in the name of Jesus Christ.

17. O God my Father, let there be divine green light concerning all my endeavors, in the name of Jesus Christ.

18. By the power in the name of Jesus Christ, I arrest every satanic agent assigned to stop me, in the name of Jesus Christ.

19. By the power in the name of Jesus Christ, I arrest every satanic agent assigned to stop my progress, in the name of Jesus Christ.

20. By the power in the name of Jesus Christ, I arrest every satanic agent assigned to stop my success, in the name of Jesus Christ.

21. By the power in the name of Jesus Christ, I arrest every satanic agent assigned to stop my promotion, in the name of Jesus Christ.

22. By the power in the name of Jesus Christ, I arrest every satanic agent assigned to stop my dreams, in the name of Jesus Christ.

23. By the power in the name of Jesus Christ, I arrest every satanic agent assigned to stop my breakthroughs, in the name of Jesus Christ.

24. Every satanic full stop assigned to detain me, I command you to disappear, in the name of Jesus Christ.

25. Any power anywhere pressing my head down; be destroyed now by the fire of God, in the name of Jesus Christ.

26. Every altar of satanic delay erected against me; be destroyed now by the fire of God, in the name of Jesus Christ.

27. Every altar of satanic delay erected against my destiny; be destroyed now by the fire of God, in the name of Jesus Christ.

28. Every altar of satanic delay erected against my fruitfulness; be destroyed now by the fire of God, in the name of Jesus Christ.

29. Every altar of satanic delay erected against my child bearing; be destroyed now by the fire of God, in the name of Jesus Christ.

30. Every altar of satanic delay erected against my promotion; be destroyed now by the fire of God, in the name of Jesus Christ.

31. Every altar of satanic delay erected against my testimonies; be destroyed now by the fire of God, in the name of Jesus Christ.

32. Every altar of satanic delay erected against the time of my celebration; be destroyed now by the fire of God, in the name of Jesus Christ.

33. I command my hidden treasures buried in secret to come forth right now, in the name of Jesus Christ.

34. I command my glory buried in secret to come forth right now, in the name of Jesus Christ.

35. I command my virtue buried in secret to come forth right now, in the name of Jesus Christ.

36. Every satanic yoke assigned to frustrate my efforts; break now by the fire of God, in the name of Jesus Christ.

37. Ancient gates blocking my inheritance; be destroyed now by the fire of God, in the name of Jesus Christ.

38. Ancient gates blocking my laughter; be destroyed now by the fire of God, in the name of Jesus Christ.

39. A miracle that cannot be doubted, manifest in my life now, in the name of Jesus Christ.

40. Glory that cannot be doubted, Father Lord, let it be given unto me, in the name of Jesus Christ.

41. Any power anywhere planning to steal my laughter, you will not escape the judgment of God, in the name of Jesus Christ.

42. Anointing for victory laughter; fall upon me now, in the name of Jesus Christ.

43. Satanic barriers erected to stop me; be destroyed right now by the fire of God, in the name of Jesus Christ.

44. Satanic strongholds erected to stop me; be destroyed right now by the fire of God, in the name of Jesus Christ.

45. O God my Father, send my Moses today. I am ready to get out of this bondage, in the name of Jesus Christ.

46. O God my Father, force my Pharaoh to release me from this slavery and let me go, in the name of Jesus Christ.

47. I refuse to leave Egypt empty handed. Let all my stolen blessings return to me now, in the name of Jesus Christ.

48. Pharaoh of my father's house planning to stop me from getting out of Egyptian bondage; you will not escape the judgment of God, in the name of Jesus Christ.

49. Every Red Sea planning to stop me from getting out of Egyptian bondage; I command you to give way, in the name of Jesus Christ.

50. Wall of Jericho planning to stop my entry to the promise land; I command you to collapse, in the name of Jesus Christ.

51. River Jordan planning to stop my entry to the promise land; I command you to be driven back, in the name of Jesus Christ.

52. Wilderness of disappointment planning to stop my advancement; I command you to give way now, in the name of Jesus Christ.

53. Wilderness of failure planning to stop my progress; I command you to give way now, in the name of Jesus Christ.

54. Wilderness of sorrow planning to stop my season of joy; I command you to disappear now, in the name of Jesus Christ.

55. Wilderness of loneliness planning to stop the fulfillment of God's promise; I command you to disappear, in the name of Jesus Christ.

56. Any power anywhere adding to my pain; you will not escape the judgment of God, in the name of Jesus Christ.

57. Any power anywhere adding to my frustration; you will not escape the judgment of God, in the name of Jesus Christ.

58. O God my Father, give me a victory that cannot be disputed, in the name of Jesus Christ.

59. I command every satanic red light in my way to be destroyed completely by the fire of God, in the name of Jesus Christ.

60. I have the life of God in me. I have the blood of Jesus all over me. I am unstoppable, in the name of Jesus Christ.

61. O God my Father, enlarge my territory to a dumbfounding degree, in the name of Jesus Christ.

62. I am moving forward to possess my throne. I shall not be stopped by household wickedness, in the name of Jesus Christ.

63. Today, I possess the spirit of Joseph. I refuse to be stuck in the pit of hopelessness; I must move forward to possess my throne, in the name of Jesus Christ.

64. I possess the spirit of Joseph. I command every chain of slavery upon me to break now. I must move forward to possess my throne, in the name of Jesus Christ.

65. I possess the spirit of Joseph. I refuse to settle for Potiphar's hospitality. I must move forward to possess my throne, in the name of Jesus Christ.

66. I possess the spirit of Joseph. I refuse to settle for Potiphar's wife offer. I must move forward to possess my throne, in the name of Jesus Christ.

67. I possess the spirit of Joseph. I refuse to trade my destiny for any satanic offer, in the name of Jesus Christ.

68. I possess the spirit of Joseph. I refuse to be distracted. I must move forward to possess my throne, in the name of Jesus Christ.

69. I possess the spirit of Joseph. I will not die in the prison. I must move forward to possess my throne, in the name of Jesus Christ.

70. I possess the spirit of Joseph. I refuse to settle for any position or title given to me in the prison. I must move forward to possess my throne, in the name of Jesus Christ.

71. I possess the spirit of Joseph. I set my slave garment on fire today; and I receive a change of clothes that fits the throne, in the name of Jesus Christ.

72. O God my Father, let my helpers have problems that only I can solve, in the name of Jesus Christ.

73. O God my Father, let my helpers remember to help me today, in the name of Jesus Christ.

74. O God my Father, let everyone see your good hands upon me and help me to ascend to my throne, in the name of Jesus Christ.

75. O God my Father, arise and convert evil plans of household wickedness against me to success, in the name of Jesus Christ.

76. O God my Father, arise and convert evil plans of unfriendly friends against me to promotion, in the name of Jesus Christ.

77. O God my Father, arise and convert evil plans of the power of darkness against me to uncommon breakthroughs, in the name of Jesus Christ.

78. O God my Father, arise and convert evil plans of the enemy against me to financial freedom, in the name of Jesus Christ.

79. O God my Father, make a way for me today where there is no way. I am ready to move forward, in the name of Jesus Christ.

80. O God my Father, let the pillar of cloud lead me by day, and the pillar of fire lead me by night. I am moving forward no matter what, in the name of Jesus Christ.

I cover my prayers in the blood of Jesus Christ. According to the Word of God, I have asked, I shall receive. I have knocked the door, it shall be opened unto me. I have sought, I shall find, in the name of Jesus Christ. It is written, "... Decree a thing, and it shall be established". As I have spoken in prayer, it shall be so. My prayers shall produce desire results. My prayers shall produce desired miracles. My prayers shall produce desired testimonies, in the name of Jesus Christ. Territorial spirit and power cannot hinder this prayer. Sins and flesh cannot hinder this prayer. It is done. It is sealed by the blood of Jesus Christ. It is delivered to me, in Jesus might name. Amen!

DAY THIRTEEN

LET YOUR ANGELS LOCATE MY BLESSINGS

Passages To Read Before You Pray:
Daniel 10:10-13, 1 Samuel 5:1-12, Hebrews 12:29,
Psalms 3, 9, 59, 69, 86

In the book of Job 22:28, the Scripture says when I decree a thing, it shall be established for me. I stand on this Scripture and decree. I have come today to fellowship with my heavenly Father, and make my requests and needs known unto Him. I cannot be hindered nor delayed because I know who I am in the Lord. I am a child of the Kingdom, born of the Spirit, redeemed by the blood of Jesus Christ. I walk in authority, living life without any apology because the power and authority has been given to me according to the Word of God in the book of Luke 9:1.

As I have come to pray today and to fellowship with my heavenly Father, I cover myself in the blood of Jesus Christ, and I put on the whole armor of God. I hereby come against every Prince of Persia that wants to hinder my prayer, I arrest you by the power in the blood of Jesus Christ, and I bind you and cast you down into the pit of hell.

I come against principalities and powers that wrestle with me and my prayers, I arrest you today by the power in the name of Jesus Christ, and I bind you and cast down into the pit of hell. I come against the rulers of the darkness of this world, against spiritual wickedness in high places, I arrest you all by the power in the name of Jesus Christ, and I bind you and cast you down into the pit of hell. I come against weakness and weariness, I

arrest you today by the power in the name of Jesus Christ, and I bind you and cast you out of my life. I come against wondering spirit and distractions, I arrest you today by the power in the name of Jesus Christ, and I bind you and cast you out of my life.

Today I receive the anointing to pray and get results, my prayers cannot be hindered nor delayed because Jesus is my Lord, I will pray today and get the desired results, I decree open heavens upon my prayers. I baptize myself in the fire of the Holy Ghost; therefore I have become too hot for the enemy to handle. My prayers today will attract divine intervention to every situation in my life; signs and wonders will follow my prayers today, testimonies will follow my prayers today and the name of God alone will be glorified, in Jesus name. Amen!

PRAYER POINTS

1. O God my Father, thank you for being my God, My Father and my friend.
2. O God my Father, thank you for the privilege to know you and the power of the resurrection of Jesus Christ.
3. O God my Father, thank you for always being there for me and with me.
4. O God my Father, thank you for the great and mighty things that you are doing in my life.
5. O God my Father, thank you for your provision and protection over me and my household.
6. O God my Father, thank you for always answering my prayers.

7. I confess my sins before you today and I ask you to forgive me on the basis of your mercy, in the name of Jesus Christ.
8. Wash me clean today O Lord by the blood of Jesus Christ.
9. I cover myself and my household with the blood of Jesus Christ.
10. My prayers today will not go in vain; my prayers will produce the desired results in the name of Jesus Christ.
11. I put on the whole armor of God.
12. By the power in the name of Jesus Christ, I overcome every attack of the enemy by the blood of Jesus Christ.
13. I overcome every spiritual conspiracy against me by the blood of Jesus Christ.
14. I overcome every joint operation of the enemy by the blood of Jesus Christ, and I scatter them by the fire of God.
15. I overcome every covert operation of the enemy by the blood of Jesus Christ, and I destroy them by the fire of God.
16. I scatter every satanic network working against me by the fire of God, in the name of Jesus Christ.
17. Any power anywhere that lets me see my blessings but will not allow me touch it, be destroyed today by the fire of God.
18. Any power anywhere that lets me see my blessings but will not allow me have it, be destroyed today by the fire of God.
19. Any power anywhere that lets me see my blessings but will not allow me to enjoy them, be destroyed today by the fire of God.

20. Any power anywhere that lets me see my miracles but will not allow me touch them, be destroyed today by the fire of God.

21. Any power anywhere that lets me see my miracles but will not allow me have them, be destroyed today by the fire of God.

22. Any power anywhere that lets me see my miracles but not allow me enjoy them, be destroyed today by the fire of God.

23. Any power anywhere that lets me see the answers to prayers but will not allow me have them, be destroyed today by the fire of God.

24. Any power anywhere that lets me see the answers to prayers but will not allow me enjoy them, be destroyed today by the fire of God.

25. Today O Lord, let every strategy of the enemy used against me fail woefully, in the name of Jesus Christ.

26. Today O Lord, let every strategy of the enemy used to rob me of my blessings fail woefully, in the name of Jesus Christ.

27. Today O Lord, let every strategy of the enemy used to hinder my prayers fail woefully, in the name of Jesus Christ.

28. Today O Lord, let every strategy of the enemy used to delay my miracles fail woefully, in the name of Jesus Christ.

29. Today O Lord, let every strategy of the enemy used to keep me in the bondage of poverty fail woefully, in the name of Jesus Christ.

30. Today O Lord, let every strategy of the enemy used to keep me in the dark fail woefully, in the name of Jesus Christ.

31. Today O Lord, let every strategy of the enemy used to intercept my breakthrough fail woefully, in the name of Jesus Christ.

32. Today O Lord, let every strategy of the enemy used to rob me of my joy fail woefully, in the name of Jesus Christ.

33. Today O Lord, let every strategy of the enemy used to take away my rest fail woefully, in the name of Jesus Christ.

34. Today O Lord, let every strategy of the enemy used to stop my progress fail woefully, in the name of Jesus Christ.

35. Today O Lord, let every strategy of the enemy used to quench the fire of God in me fail woefully, in the name of Jesus Christ.

36. Today O Lord, let every strategy of the enemy used to take away my rod of prayer fail woefully, in the name of Jesus Christ.

37. Today O Lord, let every strategy of the enemy used to make me work against myself fail woefully, in the name of Jesus Christ.

38. O God my Father, let my caged blessings break forth and come to me now, in the name of Jesus Christ.

39. O God my Father, let my blessings in the hands of the enemy become the Ark of the Covenant, and trouble them until they release my blessings, in the name of Jesus Christ.

40. O God my Father, arise and send your fire to destroy the camp of the enemy where my blessing is being held, in the name of Jesus Christ.

41. O God my Father, arise and send your fire to destroy the camp of the enemy where my miracle is being caged, in the name of Jesus Christ.

42. O God my Father, arise and send your fire to destroy the camp of the enemy where my breakthrough is being held, in the name of Jesus Christ.

43. O God my Father, arise and send your fire to destroy the camp of the enemy where they are working against my finances, in the name of Jesus Christ.

44. O God my Father, arise and send your fire to destroy the camp of the enemy where they are working against my progress, in the name of Jesus Christ.

45. O God my Father, arise and send your fire to destroy the headquarters of the enemy of my success, in the name of Jesus Christ.

46. O God my Father, arise and send your fire to destroy the headquarters of the enemy of my breakthrough, in the name of Jesus Christ.

47. O God my Father, arise and send your fire to destroy the headquarters of the enemy of my marriage, in the name of Jesus Christ.

48. O God my Father, arise and send your fire to destroy the headquarters of the enemy that wants me to die struggling, in the name of Jesus Christ.

49. O God my Father, arise and send your fire to destroy the headquarters of the enemy that wants me to die poor, in the name of Jesus Christ.

50. O God my Father, dispatch your angels to search the whole earth, to locate my blessing and bring it to me, in the name of Jesus Christ.

51. O God my Father, dispatch your angels to search the heavens, to locate my blessing and bring it to me, in the name of Jesus Christ.

52. O God my Father, dispatch your angels to search the kingdom of darkness, to locate my blessing and bring it to me, in the name of Jesus Christ.

53. O God my Father, dispatch your angels to search the warehouse of the enemy to locate my blessing and bring it to me, in the name of Jesus Christ.

54. O God my Father, dispatch your angels to search every satanic storage to locate my blessing and bring it to me, in the name of Jesus Christ.

55. O God my Father, dispatch your angels to search the oceanic kingdom of darkness to locate my blessing and bring it to me, in the name of Jesus Christ.

56. O God my Father, dispatch your angels to search the kingdom of hell to locate my blessing and bring it to me, in theme of Jesus Christ.

57. O God my Father, dispatch your angels to search the marine kingdom of darkness to locate my blessing and bring it to me, in the name of Jesus Christ.

58. O God my Father, dispatch your angels to search every area where the enemy buries glory and destiny, to locate my blessing, and bring it to me, in the name of Jesus Christ.

59. O God my Father, dispatch your angels to search every area where the enemy changes glory and destiny, to locate my blessing, and bring it to me, in the name of Jesus Christ.

60. O God my Father, dispatch your angels to search every area where the enemy destroys people's life, to locate my blessing and bring it to me, in the name of Jesus Christ.

61. O God my Father, dispatch your angels to search the camp of my household wickedness to locate my blessing, and bring it to me, in the name of Jesus Christ.

62. O God my Father, dispatch your angels to search the house of the strongman of my father's house to locate my blessing and bring it to me, in the name of Jesus Christ.

63. O God my Father, dispatch your angels to search the house of the strongman of mother's house, to locate my blessing and bring it to me, in the name of Jesus Christ.

64. O God my Father, dispatch your angels to search the house of the strongman of my place of birth, to locate my blessing and bring it to me, in Jesus name.

65. O God my Father, dispatch your angels to search the house of the strongman in the city where I live, to locate my blessing and bring it to me, in the name of Jesus Christ.

66. O God my Father, dispatch your angels to locate every satanic contractor working on my case, to retrieve my blessing and bring it to me, in the name of Jesus Christ.

67. O God my Father, dispatch your angels to locate every satanic contractor working on my case, to retrieve my stolen miracle and bring it to me, in the name of Jesus Christ.

68. O God my Father, dispatch your angels to locate every satanic contractor working on my case, to retrieve my stolen joy and bring it to me, in the name of Jesus Christ.

69. O God my Father, dispatch your angels to locate every satanic contractor working on my case, and let my stolen blessings be restored back to me, in the name of Jesus Christ.

70. O God my Father, dispatch your angels to locate every satanic contractor working on my case, and let stolen

breakthrough be restored back to me, in the name of Jesus Christ.

71. O God my Father, dispatch your angels to locate every satanic contractor working on my case, and let my lost job be restored back to me, in the name of Jesus Christ.

72. O God my Father, as from today, in the presence of my enemies I will enjoy the food that you have prepared for me, in the name of Jesus Christ.

73. O God my Father, as from today, in the presence of enemies I will enjoy my breakthroughs, in the name of Jesus Christ.

74. O God my Father, as from today, in the presence of my enemies I will have success in every area and enjoy it, in the name of Jesus Christ.

75. O God my Father, I receive my miracle today with thanksgiving, and I will enjoy every bit of it, in the name of Jesus Christ.

76. O God my Father, I receive my blessing today with thanksgiving and I will enjoy every bit of it, in the name of Jesus Christ.

77. O God my Father, I receive my financial breakthrough today with thanksgiving, and I will enjoy every bit of it, in the name of Jesus Christ.

78. O God my Father, I receive my promotion in every area today with thanksgiving, and I will enjoy every bit of it, in the name of Jesus Christ.

79. O God my Father, I receive success in every area today with thanksgiving, and I will enjoy it, in the name of Jesus Christ.

80. O God my Father, I receive the answer to my prayers today with thanksgiving, and it shall be permanent, in the name of Jesus Christ.

81. O God my Father, I receive solution to my situations today with thanksgiving, and it shall be permanent, in the name of Jesus Christ.
82. O God my Father, I receive my healing today with thanksgiving, and it shall be permanent, in the name of Jesus Christ.
83. Every satanic bottle holding my blessings, break now by the fire of God, in the name of Jesus Christ.
84. Every satanic bottle holding my miracles, break now by the fire of God, in the name of Jesus Christ.
85. Every satanic bottle holding my success, break now by the fire of God, in the name of Jesus Christ.
86. Every satanic bottle holding my finances, break now by the fire of God, in the name of Jesus Christ.
87. Every satanic bottle holding the answer to my prayers, break now by the fire of God, in the name of Jesus Christ.
88. Every satanic bottle holding my testimonies, break now by the fire of God, in the name of Jesus Christ.
89. Every satanic bottle holding my progress, break now by the fire of God, in the name of Jesus Christ.
90. Every satanic bottle holding my joy, break now by the fire of God, in the name of Jesus Christ.
91. O God my Father, enough is enough; I shall never labor in vain again, in the name of Jesus Christ.
92. O God my Father, enough is enough, I shall never lack again, in the name of Jesus Christ.
93. O God my Father, enough is enough; I shall never fail again, in the name of Jesus Christ.
94. O God my Father, enough is enough; I shall never endure shame again, in the name of Jesus Christ.

I cover my prayers in the blood of Jesus Christ. According to the Word of God, I have asked; I shall receive. I have knocked the door; it shall be opened unto me. I have sought; I shall find, in the name of Jesus Christ. It is written, "... Decree a thing, and it shall be established". As I have spoken in prayer, it shall be so. My prayers shall produce desired results. My prayers shall produce desired miracles. My prayers shall produce desired testimonies, in the name of Jesus Christ. Territorial spirit and power cannot hinder this prayer. Sins and flesh cannot hinder this prayer. It is done. It is sealed by the blood of Jesus Christ. It is delivered to me, in Jesus mighty name. Amen!

DAY FOURTEEN

IT IS MY TIME TO SHINE

Passages To Read Before You Pray:
Job 22:28, Proverbs 18:21, Isaiah 60:1-22, Psalms 19, 29, 42

In the book of Job 22:28, the Scripture says when I decree a thing, it shall be established for me. I stand on this Scripture and decree. I have come today to fellowship with my heavenly Father, and make my requests and needs known unto Him. I cannot be hindered nor delayed because I know who I am in the Lord. I am a child of the Kingdom, born of the Spirit, redeemed by the blood of Jesus Christ. I walk in authority, living life without any apology because the power and authority has been given to me according to the Word of God in the book of Luke 9:1.

As I have come to pray today and to fellowship with my heavenly Father, I cover myself in the blood of Jesus Christ, and I put on the whole armor of God. I hereby come against every Prince of Persia that wants to hinder my prayer, I arrest you by the power in the blood of Jesus Christ, and I bind you and cast you down into the pit of hell.

I come against principalities and powers that wrestle with me and my prayers, I arrest you today by the power in the name of Jesus Christ, and I bind you and cast down into the pit of hell. I come against the rulers of the darkness of this world, against spiritual wickedness in high places, I arrest you all by the power in the name of Jesus Christ, and I bind you and cast you down into the pit of hell. I come against weakness and weariness, I arrest you today by the power in the name of Jesus Christ, and I

bind you and cast you out of my life. I come against wondering spirit and distractions, I arrest you today by the power in the name of Jesus Christ, and I bind you and cast you out of my life.

Today I receive the anointing to pray and get results, my prayers cannot be hindered nor delayed because Jesus is my Lord, I will pray today and get the desired results, I decree open heavens upon my prayers. I baptize myself in the fire of the Holy Ghost; therefore I have become too hot for the enemy to handle. My prayers today will attract divine intervention to every situation in my life; signs and wonders will follow my prayers today, testimonies will follow my prayers today and the name of God alone will be glorified, in Jesus name. Amen!

PRAYER POINTS

1. O God my Father, thank you for being my God, My Father and my friend.
2. O God my Father, thank you for the privilege to know you and the power of the resurrection of Jesus Christ.
3. O God my Father, thank you for always being there for me and with me.
4. O God my Father, thank you for the great and mighty things that you are doing in my life.
5. O God my Father, thank you for your provision and protection over me and my household.
6. O God my Father, thank you for always answering my prayers.

7. I confess my sins before you today and I ask you to forgive me on the basis of your mercy, in the name of Jesus Christ.

8. Wash me clean today O Lord by the blood of Jesus Christ.

9. I cover myself and my household with the blood of Jesus Christ.

10. My prayers today will not go in vain; my prayers will produce the desired results in the name of Jesus Christ.

11. It is my time to shine; I command every curse of stagnancy to break in Jesus name.

12. It is my time to shine; I command every curse of failure to break.

13. It is my time to shine; I command every curse of debt to break.

14. It is my time to shine; I command every curse of backwardness to break.

15. It is my time to shine; I command every curse of sickness to break.

16. It is my time to shine; I command every curse of emptiness to break.

17. It is my time to shine, I command every curse of almost there to break.

18. It is my time to shine; I command every curse of poverty to break.

19. It is my time to shine; I command every curse of nakedness to break.

20. It is my time to shine; I command every curse of last minute denial to break.

21. Every opposition against my breakthroughs is cancelled, in Jesus' name.
22. Every opposition against my success is cancelled, in Jesus' name.
23. Every conspiracy to hold me down at the bottom of the ladder, scatter, in Jesus name.
24. Every conspiracy of the enemy to keep me in bondage, scatter.
25. I refuse to settle for the offer of the enemies.
26. I break every curse holding me back from fulfilling my destiny.
27. I break every curse delaying my success.
28. Every curse upon my life delaying my promotion, break.
29. Every curse upon my life delaying my breakthrough, break.
30. Every curse upon my life that has determined to make me a loser, break now.
31. I break every agreement that I have made to destroy my life.
32. I terminate every contract signed by anyone to make me a slave.
33. It is my time to shine, I command the best of God in me to manifest by fire.
34. It is my time to shine; I command all my dreams to come alive.
35. Father Lord, let the greatness that you have put in me come out by fire and prove my enemies wrong.
36. Father Lord, let the best in me shine forth and put my enemies to shame.
37. I receive special anointing today to achieve my goals.
38. I receive special anointing today to fulfill my dreams.

39. Father Lord, let your mighty hands rest upon me today and bring the best out of me.
40. Father Lord, set my finances free today from the hands of my enemies.
41. Let my divine helpers see the best of God in me.
42. My enemies shall bow before my star like the case of Joseph.
43. I refuse to cooperate with the plan of the enemy against my life.
44. I cancel and destroy every demonic agenda against my life.
45. Every mouth speaking evil against me shall not prosper in Jesus name.
46. I refuse to cooperate with the plan of the enemy to make me a beggar.
47. I refuse to cooperate with the plan of the enemy to make me a failure.
48. I refuse to cooperate with the plan of the enemy to make me a loser.
49. I refuse to cooperate with the plan of the enemy to make me homeless.
50. I refuse to cooperate with the plan of the enemy to make me poor.
51. I receive anointing and power to receive and manage my blessings.
52. I receive anointing and power to get and control wealth.
53. I receive anointing and power to receive and keep my breakthroughs.
54. Today shall mark the beginning of my success.
55. Today shall mark the beginning of my breakthroughs.
56. I command the best of God in me to produce greatness.
57. I command the best of God in me to make ways for me.

58. I command every area of my life to be productive.
59. Today shall mark the beginning of my greatness.
60. I shall not lack any good thing.
61. I shall live to fulfill my purpose.
62. I shall live to enjoy the fruits of my labor.
63. Every evil handwriting against me shall not stand, be erased by the blood of Jesus.

I cover my prayers in the blood of Jesus Christ. According to the Word of God, I have asked; I shall receive. I have knocked the door; it shall be opened unto me. I have sought; I shall find, in the name of Jesus Christ. It is written, "… Decree a thing, and it shall be established". As I have spoken in prayer, it shall be so. My prayers shall produce desired results. My prayers shall produce desired miracles. My prayers shall produce desired testimonies, in the name of Jesus Christ. Territorial spirit and power cannot hinder this prayer. Sins and flesh cannot hinder this prayer. It is done. It is sealed by the blood of Jesus Christ. It is delivered to me, in Jesus mighty name. Amen!

I Must Win This Battle

I Must Win This Battle offers a hands-on training self-deliverance process and prayers. It covers over 2000 prayer points focusing on how to remove unpleasant and unwanted situations of life. Battle of life is a must win for every child of God and this book shows how to, in a very simple and effective way. It is a must have for every household.

Let There Be A Change

"Let There Be A Change" is a must have Personal Deliverance prayer book that will transform your life and bring restoration into every area of your life. What is Deliverance? Deliverance means to loose the bounds of wickedness. A lot of people are under the bondage of wickedness. If you look at the lives of many people, you will discover a wide array of wicked occurrences. If your life is surrounded by wicked mysterious happenings, you need to seek deliverance as soon as possible. Deliverance centers on the destruction of the yoke of the enemy. A yoke is anything that hinders or sets you back. Whatever sets you back from moving forward in your life is a yoke. God's will is that you move forward and attain divine goals set for your life. When the contrary happens, there is a bondage hanging above your life. Deliverance is to break curses and evil covenants. The ancestors of many people were cursed and the curses have flown down the family line. For example, if a person struggles without any tangible achievement in life, there is a problem somewhere.

Earth Moving Prayers

"I have seen the affliction of my people, and have heard their cry by reason of their enemies and tormentors, for I know their sorrows; and I have come down to deliver them out of the hand of the wicked and unrepentant enemies. And I will surely bring to pass my plans and counsels concerning them." This is the Word of the Lord that gave birth to this Anointed Prayer Book, "EARTH-MOVING PRAYERS". Earth-Moving Prayers is a highly anointed deliverance prayer book that will transform your life, and set you free from any form of bondage or captivity you may find yourself. Over 600 pages of mountain moving and yoke destroying prayer points. Over 5300 problems solving and solution finding prayer points prepared by the Holy Ghost to set you free. If you are ready to take your life back from that terrible situation, this book is for you, a must have for every household.

Total Deliverance – Volume 1

"Why would you pay for a debt that you did not owe? Why would you have to be what the enemies want your life to be? The plan of God for you is to live freely and prosper as He has promised in the Scriptures. You do not have to pay for the sins of your parents or ancestors; you don't have to go through what they went through, your life is different and your case is different. If you can just believe, the Bible says, "You will see the glory of God." – John 11:40

This book is loaded with prayers that will transform your life, deliver you from ancestral curses, generational and foundational curses, self-inflicted curses, break yokes and destroy bondages no matter how long it's been there."

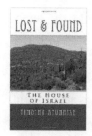

Lost & Found: The House of Israel

Lost & Found "The House of Israel" offers detailed information about the past, present and future of the House of Israel. Jacob released special blessings upon two of his children, he gave Joseph the Birthright and Judah the Kingdom. God made covenant with David that he will always have a son on his throne and his throne will be everlasting. In this book, you will discover where the throne of David is currently and how it got there. It is a must for every Bible student.

Divine Intervention

Deliverance centers on the destruction of the yoke of the enemy. A yoke is anything that hinders or sets you back. Whatever sets you back from moving forward in your life is a yoke. God's will is that you move forward and attain divine goals set for your life. When the contrary happens, there is a bondage hanging above your life.

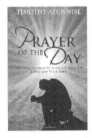

Prayer of The Day – Volume 1

How wonderful would it be to start your day with joy and end it with great success? The Spirit of the Lord led me to write Prayer of the Day, a wonderful, daily spiritual vitamin. He promised that this book would touch and change many lives and situations for the better as people began to commit every day to the hands of God, for He knows the beginning and ending. Prayer is communion with God. Through prayer we actually experience relationship with God. The quality of our prayer life determines the quality of our relationship with God. I promise you, in the name of the Lord, that you will experience the power of God, great deliverance and a move of the Holy Spirit in your life as you join millions of people across the globe in prayer every morning before you start your day.

Prayer of The Day – Volume 2

How wonderful would it be to start your day with joy and end it with great success? The Spirit of the Lord led me to write Prayer of the Day, a wonderful, daily spiritual vitamin. He promised that this book would touch and change many lives and situations for the better as people began to commit every day to the hands of God, for He knows the beginning and ending. Prayer is communion with God. Through prayer we actually experience relationship with God. The quality of our prayer life determines the quality of our relationship with God. I promise you, in the name of the Lord, that you will experience the power of God, great deliverance and a move of the Holy Spirit in your life as you join millions of people across the globe in prayer every morning before you start your day.

Overcoming Self

Sunday School manual

The King Is Coming

The King Is Coming teaches the End-Times messages and prophecies. It is very accurate and easy to understand. It shows the application of the Word of God to current affairs, and establishing the truth of what is happening in world today in the Scripture. It is written to prepare the Saints for that Glorious Hope and for the End-Times assignments (End-Times Revival).

The Fruit of The Spirit

Fruit of the Spirit is mentioned in several areas of the Bible. However, the most applicable passage is Galatians 5:22-23 where Paul actually lists out the fruits. Paul used this list to show the contrast between a Godly character and one that is focused on fleshly concerns. These are not just individual "fruits" (attributes) from which to pick and choose. Rather, the fruit of the Spirit is one ninefold "fruit" that characterizes all who truly walk in the Holy Spirit. In order to understand the fruit of the Spirit, we must first understand who the Spirit is, what He does and how He helps us live our lives pleasing to God. The questions are: What are the Fruits of the Spirit? How can you develop them? What does that mean for you? What fruits of the Spirit do you have?

The Parables of Jesus Christ

A parable is a story in which a real and earthly thing is used to parallel or illustrate a spiritual or heavenly thing. Such a story acts as a "riddle" that both veils and reveals all at once -- veiling the spiritual behind words that reveal the earthly and which can be penetrated to reach the spiritual by those "who have ears to hear." Jesus tells us that He spoke in parables precisely to veil and reveal, to speak, in a sense, "secretly" while not in secret at all.

The Miracles of Jesus Christ

Understanding the story of the healing and miracles of Jesus Christ. Christ came into the world, not only as God's personal representative on earth, but as God manifest in flesh. He was Himself a miracle in human form, and His miraculous works are bound up inseparably with His life. "The blind receive their sight and the lame walk; the lepers are cleansed and the deaf hear; the dead are raised up and the poor have the gospel preached to them". His miracles provided proof of who He was.

Bible Study: The Book of Exodus

This Bible study is designed as an expository study of the Book of Exodus, taking the student through large portions of this Old Testament book with cross references to other portions of Scripture. The purpose is to assist the student in gaining a greater comprehension of the biblical teaching contained in the Book of Exodus with an emphasis on practical application. This study presents introductory information about the Book of Exodus followed by twenty-two lessons devoted to an in-depth study of the biblical text. The student will begin by exploring a portion of Exodus with the help of a series of exploratory questions. There will then follow an in-depth study of the passage, guided by an expositional commentary on the text. The student should prepare for his study by asking the Holy Spirit to enlighten his mind and open his heart to receive not only the teaching of Scripture but Christ Himself as He is presented in the Scriptures.

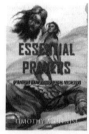

Essential Prayers:
(Prayers That Bring Total Victory)

Essential Prayers is an anointed prayer book that touches every aspect of life. It offers ways to make prayers more personal and powerful, and how to establish a practice of prayer that works. Essential Prayers is for every Christian home, it will surely transform your prayer life and reshape your entire outlook of life.

Essential Prayers addresses your personal situations, it provides prayers for marriage restoration, total victory, financial release, deliverance from addiction, prayer against problems started in childhood, foundational problems, prayer for singles, prayer against ancestral debt-collectors, prayer for signs and wonders, and many more.

We are given the authority and power to take over, not to be run over. If you fail to take over, you'll be run over. Essential Prayers offers step-by-step prayer guidelines to take over and possess your possessions.

PRAYER CDs by TIMOTHY ATUNNISE

1. Pray Before You Start Your Day
2. Pray Before You Go To Bed
3. Overcoming Impossibilities
4. Prayer To Overcome Poverty
5. Prayer To Break Evil Cycles
6. Prayer To Stop Demonic Activities
7. Prayer For Business Prosperity
8. Secret of Finding God's Rest
9. Spiritual House Cleansing
10. Take Your Life Back By Force
11. Prayer To Overcome Limitations
12. Prayer To Cancel Untimely Death
13. Prayer To Break Curses of Poverty & Empty Pocket
14. Prayer For Victory Over Bad Dreams
15. Prayer For Uncommon Favor
16. Prayer For Supernatural Breakthroughs
17. Prayer To Break Ungodly Soul-Ties
18. Prayer To Overcome Financial Setbacks
19. Prayer To Destroy The Works of The Devil
20. Prayer To Overturn Stubborn Situations
21. Prayer To Close Evil Chapters
22. Prayer For Instant Miracles
23. Shaping Your Children's Future
24. Prayer For Restoration
25. I Must Win This Battle
26. The Secret of Knowing God

DELIVERANCE PRAYER CDs by TIMOTHY ATUNNISE

1. Prayer For Self-Deliverance
2. Healing The Wounded Heart
3. Prevention & Deliverance From Cancer
4. Deliverance From Evil Covenant
5. Deliverance From The Devourer
6. Deliverance & Healing Prayer
7. Identify Your Spiritual Territory (Parts 1 & 2)
8. Exercise Spiritual Authority
9. Casting Out Spirits   (Parts 1 & 2)
10. Curses & How To Deal With Them   (Parts 1 & 2)
11. How Demons Enter & Oppress People (Parts 1 & 2)
12. Deliverance From Jezebel's Spirit
13. Defeating The Strongman
14. Deliverance From The Terrible
15. Deliverance From Curses of Last-Minute Failure
16. Deliverance From Curses of Rejection

WORSHIP CDs

1. Christocentric – Worship Songs
2. I Am That I Am
3. Yahweh Reigns

Note

Made in the USA
Las Vegas, NV
28 December 2023